The
Biography and Genealogy of

Captain John Johnson

from Roxbury, Massachusetts

~~~

An Uncommon Man in the Commonwealth of
the Massachusetts Bay Colony
1630-1659

Gerald Garth Johnson

HERITAGE BOOKS
2008

HERITAGE BOOKS
AN IMPRINT OF HERITAGE BOOKS, INC.

Books, CDs, and more—Worldwide

For our listing of thousands of titles see our website
at
www.HeritageBooks.com

Published 2008 by
HERITAGE BOOKS, INC.
Publishing Division
100 Railroad Ave. #104
Westminster, Maryland 21157

Other Books by the Author:

*Ancestors and Descendants of Ira Johnson and
Abigail (Furbush) Johnson from 1590-2003*

*Puritan Children in Exile: The Effects of the Puritan Concepts of the Original Sin,
Death, Salvation,and Grace upon the Children and Grandchildren of the
Puritan Emigrants Leading to the Collapse of the Puritan Period*

The Diaries of Nancy A. Brown and William H. Brown of Edwards, New York

International Standard Book Numbers
Paperbound: 978-0-7884-1678-1
Clothbound: 978-0-7884-7196-4

CONTENTS

CONTENTS

CONTENTS

v

PREFACE

Captain Edward Johnson of Woburn, Massachusetts is quoted as saying, "to write the History of John Johnson would fill a volume, and his worth as one of the founders of the government of the colonies of Massachusetts is too well-known to be recorded here." [in the History of Essex County, Massachusetts with Biographical Sketches, Volume II, published in 1888 by D. Hamilton Hurd.] Edward Johnson goes on to describe the subject of this book, Captain John Johnson, as "the Survayor Generall of the Armes of the Country as an Undanted Spirit. And, one who was very well qualified for the work [of Surveyor General of the Arms] ready at all times to put the General Court in mind of keeping their store renewed by fresh supply" [of powder and other military supplies.] From a more contemporary person, Thomas Kozachek, Editor, *Newbury Street Press*, wrote to the author in a private letter on May 12, 1999 that "setting this figure (John Johnson) into an historical narrative is a worthwhile project."

It is my hope that this book is an effort toward the volume that Captain Edward Johnson suggested, and setting this figure [John Johnson] in a historical narrative is as worthwhile as Thomas Kozacheck of the *Newbury Street Press* wrote.

Between the years of 1629 and 1640, slightly less than 15,000 emigrants came from England bound for America....the **New** England. The author presents Captain John Johnson as a typical, yet perhaps not so typical but at least representative, of the people who were motivated to leave their homeland and venture into the unknown and uncharted land of America. Family, as well as historians, will be pleased with the newly found information about John Johnson, where he lived, where his children were born and baptized, who his wives were, his religious beliefs, his work, his relationships with other relatives and friends, as well as get a glimpse of his leadership in the Massachusetts Bay Colony, the Ancient and Honorable Artillery Company, and the Plymouth Colony. Further, examination of the villages and towns of Ware and Great Amwell, Hertfordshire, England provides insight into the type of life John Johnson and his first wife, Mary Heath Johnson led. In addition to learning about the times of the 1600's, readers can achieve a sense of the character of John Johnson as he dealt with family, civic, military, and religious issues.

In order to provide the environment of the times, the author has included information about the religion between 1590 and 1630, Puritanism, the Church of England, as well as the political upheaval in England between 1550 and 1630, King Charles II, and taxation.

Further insight and knowledge is gained from the inclusion of facts about the trip across the Atlantic Ocean, the formation of Roxbury, Massachusetts, and the day-to-day responsibilities and events in the life of John Johnson and his family.

The author, who has visited the towns and villages of Captain John Johnson in England, and who has researched all of the usual, unusual, and new sources of information both here in America and abroad in England, has discovered information about John Johnson never before printed.

An enormous debt is owed to family members, other individuals, and institutions for their helpfulness and their tolerance while the author was in the throes of research, writing, and re-writing. With the greatest gratitude, I thank the following: Karlene Johnson Messer for her constant support and technical assistance, Nancy Ticknor Johnson who gave up her dining room again and who allowed me the freedom to search, research, and travel, Cesar Augusto Johnston for inspiring me to additional research, Dr. Roger Thompson of East Anglia University for his helpful comments, Mr. John McCauley of the Ancient and Honorable Artillery of Massachusetts, and, Mrs. Beryl Crawley, AGRA, of Welwyn Garden City, Hertfordshire, England who was probably overwhelmed by the scores and scores of letters requesting research assistance. I am especially indebted to LeAnne M. Johnson Shaw who spent many days proof-reading the various drafts of this book. Without the accuracy of her help, the past of John Johnson and the Colonial Period could not have been assembled properly.

Nickole Anne Messer Quackenbush generously provided computer technical support regarding the page layout, pagination, and index of this book so that it was "reader friendly." Thank you Nicky!

Miriam Johnson, Salem, Oregon Public Library, gets special recognition for her assistance in acquiring resource books through the inter-library loan program. She is a jewel.

In addition, I thank the staffs of the following institutions in England and in America: Chelmsford Record Office, Hertfordshire Record Office, Lincolnshire Record Office, Essex Record Office, Massachusetts Historical Society, Massachusetts State Archives, New England Historic Genealogical Society, Society of Genealogists Library, University of London Library, Willamette University Hatfield Library, University of Oregon Knight Library, Reed College Library, and the American Antiquarian Society Library.

Grateful acknowledgment goes to Mr. Douglas Richardson, a genealogist from Chandler, Arizona who specializes in the records of England and New England. Richardson assisted in deciphering the handwriting of a few of the Seventeenth Century documents and records of John Johnson so that they could be meaningfully included in this book.

Lastly, many thanks to Simon J. Skudder, NHD, of Bristol, England, though he determined that he was not even remotely related to the Johnson Family, assisted with great determination and expertise in evaluating various records in libraries and Record Offices in England. He is a true friend who is greatly respected and admired.

By no means, does the author believe that this study ends all research about Captain John Johnson. It is my hope, however, that further research will be enhanced by the efforts of this endeavor.

What follows then is an unfolding of the story of Captain John Johnson as "*An Uncommon Man in the Commonwealth of the Massachusetts Bay Colony, 1630-1659.*"

Gerald Garth Johnson, Ph.D.
March 13, 2000, Salem, Oregon

ILLUSTRATIONS AND MAPS

Figure 1
Greater East Anglia
Mobility and Migration © UMP, 1994 Used by Permission

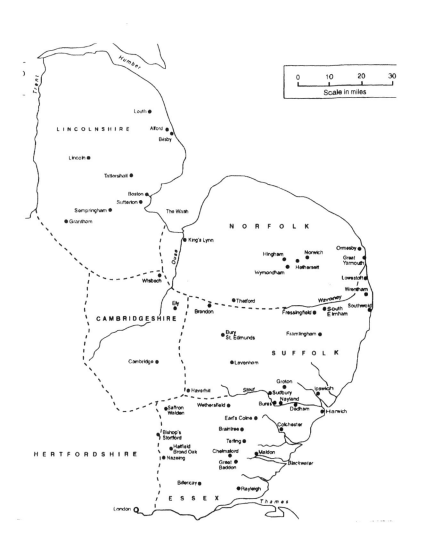

Figure 2
Map of county of Hertfordshire, England
History of Ware, © 1986 by Edith Hunt.
Mrs. Hunt left no known relatives.

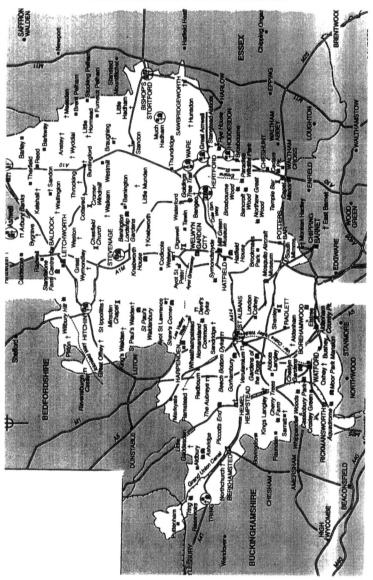

Figure 3
Map of Ware, Hertfordshire, England
History of Ware, © 1986 by Edith Hunt.
Mrs. Hunt left no known relatives.

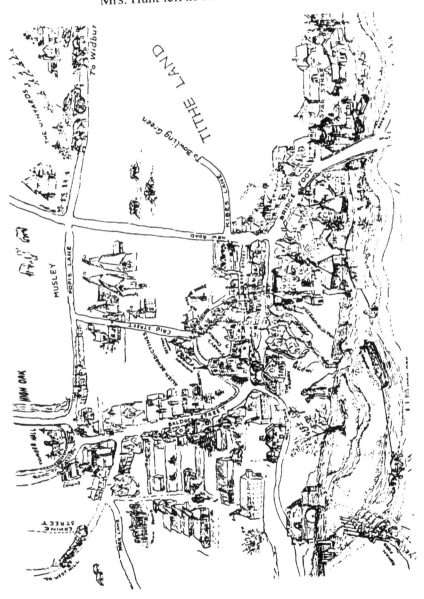

Figure 4
St. Mary's Church, Ware, England
History of Ware, © 1986 by Edith Hunt.
Mrs. Hunt left no known relatives.

ST. MARY'S CHURCH, WARE

Print by J. Dibdin. 1849, from the drawings of Geo. Godwin, architect.
(These original sketches are in the possession of the author.)

Figure 5
The River Lea (Lee), Ware, England
Photo courtesy of Mrs. Beryl Crawley

Figure 6
Map of Great Amwell, Hertfordshire, England
The Parish Register and Tithing Book of Thomas Hassall of Amwell. © Dr. Stephen Doree, 1989. Used by permission.

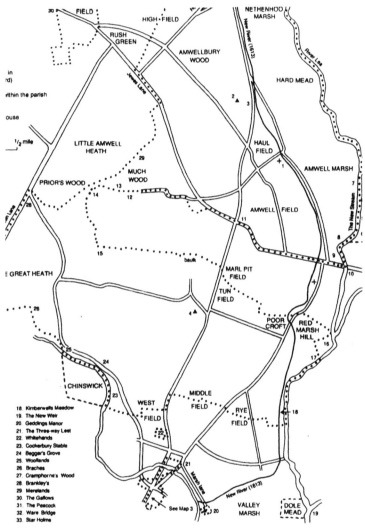

18. Kimberwells Meadow
19. The New Weir
20. Geddings Manor
21. The Three-way Leat
22. Whitehands
23. Cockerbury Stable
24. Beggar's Grove
25. Woollands
26. Braches
27. Cramphorne's Wood
28. Brankley's
29. Merelands
30. The Gallows
31. The Peacock
32. Ware Bridge
33. Star Holme

Figure 7
St. John the Baptist Church, Great Amwell,
Hertfordshire, England
Photo Courtesy of Mrs. Beryl Crawley

Figure 8
Typical Military Dress of the 17th Century
Photo source, unknown

Figure 9
Course of the Winthrop Fleet
The Winthrop Fleet © Genealogical
Publishing Company, 1983. Used by Permission

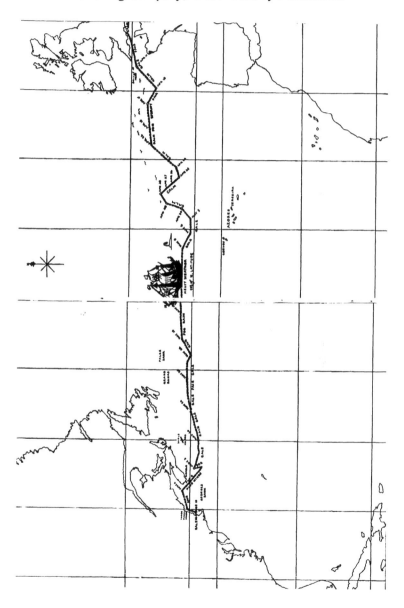

Figure 10
Stained glass window, Rev. John Cotton
Bidding farewell to Winthrop Fleet
Photo courtesy of David E. Johnson

Figure 11
New England, 1630-1650
Photo used by permission of City of Boston

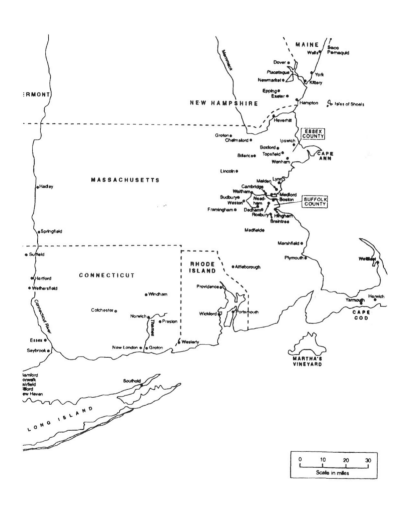

Figure 12
Massachusetts Bay, 1630-1642, Roxbury
Photo used by permission of City of Boston

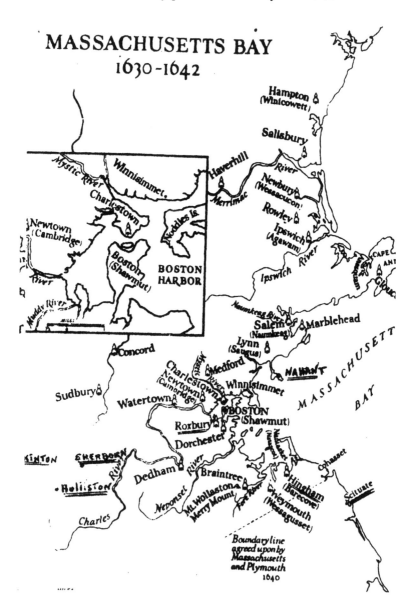

Figure 13
Shawmut, now Boston, 1630
Photo used by permission. City of Boston

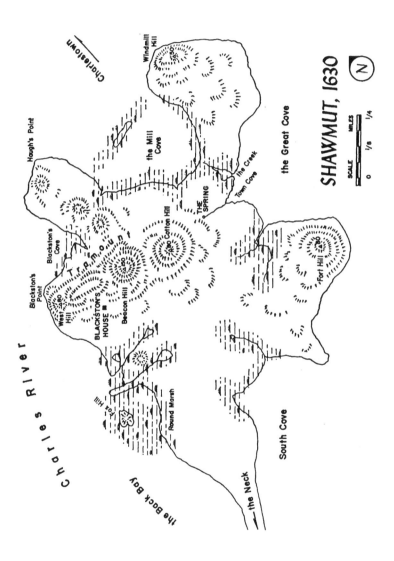

Figure 14
Roxbury, Massachusetts
Photo used by permission. City of Boston

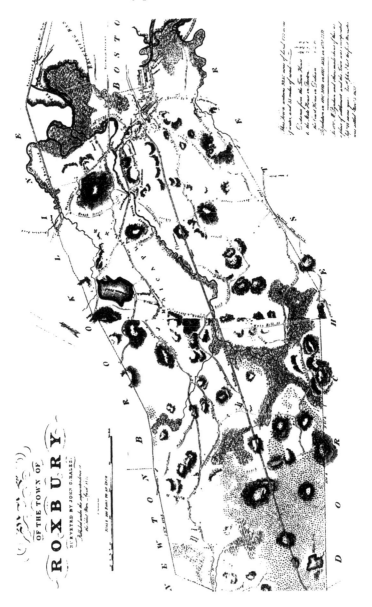

Figure 15
First Church of Roxbury (now 4th Church built)
Photo courtesy of Tercentenary Committee, Roxbury, MA

Figure 16
Boston Bay showing Roxbury at the end of "Boston Neck"
Photo used by permission. City of Boston

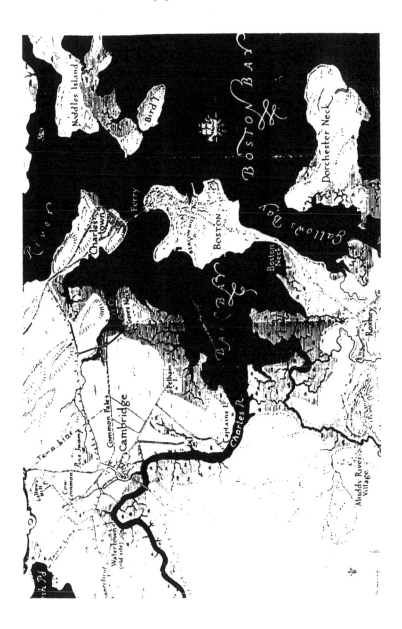

Figure 17
The First Burying Ground (Eliot Burying Ground)
in Roxbury in 1903
Photo used by permission. City of Boston

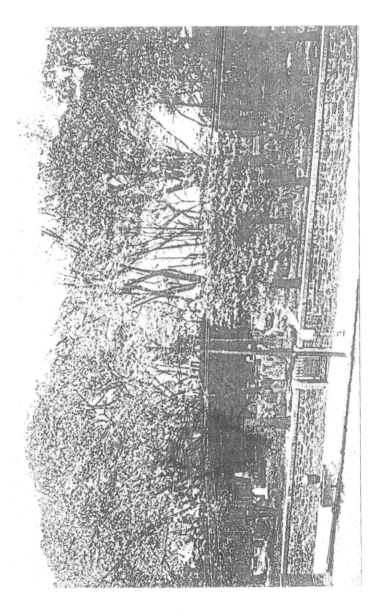

Figure 18
The First Burying Ground of Roxbury
(now called Eliot Burying Ground) in 2000
Photo courtesy of Gerald G. Johnson

INTRODUCTION

Seventeenth-century settlements in America were established by people not for one or two reasons, but for a variety of justifications representing singular and multiple motivations for migration.

Much of the written history of early Colonial America has been primarily an examination of the society and culture of the emigrants. Of particular focus has been the profound conservative religious culture of the colonists. Some other literature has focused upon the study of ancestral residence in England as well as age, gender, commercial interests, education, and professions. A recent trend has been to examine groups of emigrants ranging from 700 to over 2,000 families and single voyagers.

New England, more than anywhere else, was representative of a society patterned after the culture the founders of America left in England. With the exception of religion, the colonies in New England had similar structure politically and socially to communities in England. There was considerable control by the colonists over illegal and immoral activities of community residents for the first one hundred years.

The main difference, however, between the emigrants to America and their English counterparts, was their powerful and almost obsessive religious ideology. The quest for freedom probably led to tolerances, which some now would say was the beginning of the end of an American society that the founding fathers had hoped for. But it was this fervent ideology that led to the United States Constitution ultimately recognizing the right and the strength of one's individual thoughts, practices, and the pursuit of happiness.

Because of the discrepancies in research performed by early writers such as Pope, Torrey, Savage, Banks, and others, the author of this material personally went to England in March 1998 to visit the English towns and villages of ancestor Captain John Johnson of Roxbury, Massachusetts.

Much attention for this material is based upon newly found pamphlets, articles, books, documents, and other records both in England and in America.

Understanding the background of the mobility and freedom to migrate to America is essential in understanding the emigrant and his life in England prior to the founding of the Massachusetts Bay Colony. Correction of previously provided information about Captain John Johnson is a fundamental goal of the author since much of the available information in book form, through the Internet, and in LDS History Centers, has been speculative to say the least.

In summary, the purposes of this book about Captain John Johnson are to:

    (1)   Bring forth into one document, all that has been found in the available literature about John Johnson,

    (2)   Cite material that has never before been cited in any publication about John Johnson,

    (3)   Provide visual illustrations and maps that before had not been provided about the places John Johnson lived and worshipped,

    (4)   Add archival material heretofore left non-translated in Latin that describes John Johnson and his ancestors, and,

    (5)   Provide correction to information previously written about Captain John Johnson of Roxbury, MA.

CHAPTER ONE

THE PURITANS AND THEIR SOCIETY

"I will make them conform or I will harry them out of the land." [1] This was the threat that King James I of England (1603-1625) made to the religious dissenters when they asked him to purify the State Church of England of certain Roman Catholic ceremonies and practices, which had not been removed from the Church of England. While King James I was autocratic and totally intolerant of the Puritan movement, he was considered to be a wise and determined leader. This was because of his effort to unite the warring tribes of Scotland (when he was King James VI of Scotland); forming the British Empire; and, having the Bible translated into English, the native tongue of the common people. [2]

The first group of dissenters, called Separatists, had left England in 1608 for Amsterdam, Holland to escape persecution by the Crown of England. But by 1620, about half of those who moved to Holland decided to immigrate to America. History now refers to these first emigrants as the Pilgrims. They came to America in the ship, *The Mayflower*.

Most of the Pilgrims were purists made up of farmers and other individuals with very conservative leanings. In many ways it was an ill-fated trip in comparison to the Massachusetts Bay Colony Company of 1630. First of all, the Pilgrims did not plan their emigration at the time of year that would allow for planting and the erection of dwellings. They arrived December 21, 1620. Secondly, this Mayflower group did not plan the diversity of the colony or company to adequately accommodate the needs of the new community and to sustain it. Lastly, they intended and to be isolated and did not take into account for other possible emigration. Thus, their "Mayflower Compact" only affected those in the Plymouth Colony.

1

Half of the Plymouth Colony, as it is now called, perished in the first winter of emigration. But the remaining survivors were able to establish the Colony and keep it separate from Colonies that came later.

While the Pilgrims are given credit in much of the Colonial Period literature, it was the 1630-1660 group of emigrants many of whom were called the Puritans that refined the laws for self-government and eventually recognized the rights of the individual…predecessors for a democracy. At the time, however, they did not know that their society would lead to the freedoms inherent in a democracy. The Puritans remained staunchly rigid about liberalizing their own theocracy, and firmly stayed intolerant about recognizing Quakers, Baptists, and Catholics, to name a few.

But it was the Puritans and the Massachusetts Bay Colony who had the foresight to develop legislation for a larger entity. This eventually affected the whole of New England and that of America. The American Culture of today is because of the Puritans and, in some cases, in spite of the Puritan rigidity.

The Puritan and Pilgrim demands to King James I were a result of the lack of changes made to the Church of England by King Henry VIII who served England from 1509-1547. King Henry VIII had made himself head of the State Church of England when he could not achieve a Roman Catholic annulment of his marriage to Catherine by Pope Clement VII who had not produced a male heir. Some think that religious freedom as we know it today is a by-product of King Henry's obsession with producing a male heir. Catherine of Aragon failed to produce the male heir and the need to maintain royal legitimacy forced King Henry to seek the annulment of the marriage in order to marry Anne Boleyn

The Reformation that was begun by Martin Luther in 1517 may have set the stage for the changes demanded by the Puritans 15 years later in England. But the continental Reformation did not really find favor in England. The difference perhaps was that the break from Roman Catholicism was accomplished through the 137 laws passed by King Henry's Reformation Parliament in 1529. Actually, King Henry VIII was highly critical of the efforts of Martin Luther to have a debate over the legitimacy of the sale of indulgences by Archbishop Albert of Brandenburg as well as the discussion of the validity of the other 94 theses suggested by Luther. King Henry VIII never adopted any Protestant doctrines himself. But some of the Anglican Archbishops and clergy were highly influenced by the Reformation on the European continent. Thus, the time was ripe for further "English Reformation" of its own State Church by the people themselves.

The Puritans, as they came to be known by 1556, were not satisfied with the slight alterations made by King Henry VIII to the Roman Catholic liturgy to make the Church of England more acceptable to the English.

Believing that there was not going to be a significant change in the English Church, they began discussing how they wanted the Church of England to be. And, if changes were not possible, they would form a Church of their design. In fact, the Puritans came to believe that they were the "Chosen People of God" and were determined to have a true, pure Church that represented a full Reformation as well as found a New Jerusalem or New Israel---a new city upon a hill in the midst of the Wilderness. [3]

The religious struggle continued to cause strife in England especially during the five-year reign of Catholic Queen Mary I (daughter of King Henry VIII who abandoned the Church of England in favor of the Roman Church.)

Because the Puritan movement was made up of prominent clergy and intellectuals from Cambridge University, the East Anglia counties of England, and other educated individuals, many early religious and political Puritans were exiled or caused to go into hiding. Many Puritans died for their faith. [4]

The Massachusetts Bay Colony Charter, originally known as the Cambridge Agreement, which was carefully crafted by Governor

John Winthrop and others, provided the framework for the colonization for the plantation in New England but established the right to be free of rule by England through a vice-regal dictatorship proposed by King Charles and Archbishop Laud.

The Massachusetts Bay Company, originally designed to be like the Virginia Company, would be a corporation established in England and to be administered by the English in all of the affairs of the colony. The difference was that the Charter transferred the whole governance to the signers and further established that the Charter was to remain in New England. It was, then, essentially a plantation run by Puritans. The purpose of this drastic and probably illegal action was to secure the enterprise from interference by the King, his government, and others hostile to it. By taking the Charter to New England, the Puritans ensured that they alone would control the Company and the colony, for the Charter was the instrument that gave Massachusetts its governmental structure. [5]

The Cambridge Agreement
(Supplied by the Winthrop Society)

Upon due consideration of the state of the Plantation now in hand for New England, wherein we, whose names are hereunto subscribed, have engaged our-selves, and having weighed the greatness of the work in regard of the consequence, God's glory and the Church's good; as also in regard of the difficulties and discouragements which in all probabilities must be forecast upon the prosecution of this business; considering withal that this whole adventure grows upon the joint confidence we have in each other's fidelity and resolution herein, so as no man of us would have adventured it without assurance of the rest; now, for the better encouragement of ourselves and others that shall join with us in this action, and to the end that every man may without scruple dispose of his estate and affairs as may best fit his preparation for this voyage; it is fully and faithfully AGREED amongst us, and every one of us doth hereby freely and sincerely promised and bind himself, in the word of a Christian, and in the presence of God, who in the searcher of all hearts, that we will so really endeavour the prosecution of this work, as by God's assistance, we will be ready in our persons, and with such of our several families as are to go with us, and such provision as we are able conveniently to furnish ourselves withal, to embark for the said Plantation by the first of March next, at such port or ports of this land as shall be agreed upon by the Company, to the end to pass the seas (under God's protection) to inhabit and continue in New England: Provided always, that before the last of September next, the whole Government, together with the patent for the said Plantation, be first, by an order of Court, legally transferred and established to remain with us and others which shall inhabit upon the said Plantation; and provided also, that if any shall be hindered by such just and inevitable let or other cause, to be allowed by three parts of four of these whose names are hereunto subscribed, then such persons, for such times and during such lets, to be discharge of this bond. And we do further promise, every one for himself, that shall fail to be ready through his own default by the day appointed, to pay for every day's default the sum of L 3, to the use of the rest of the Company who shall be ready by the same day and time.

(Signed)

Richard Saltonstall
Thomas Dudley
William Vassall
Nicholas West

Isaac Johnson
John Humfrey
Thomas Sharpe
Increase Nowell
John Winthrop
William Pinchon
Kellam Browne
William Cobron

While there is always the fear of understating the importance of other reasons why the Puritans came to America, the Puritans who came to America in 1630 and thereafter had many of the following characteristics: [6,7,8]

- Disliked the robes, religious images, music in the Church, written prayers, and pictures;

- Disliked the ritual of the Church of England as being "too Catholic";

- Disliked all Roman Catholic practices which could not be supported by Scripture;

- Disliked certain celebrations and fasts such as Christmas, Easter, All Saints' Day, St. Valentine's Day, and other popular Catholic holy days;

- Wanted religious freedom; ability to form "pure" Churches as they believed rather than dictated from Church hierarchy;

- Believed that religious life and civic life were one and the same; thus a "Bible Commonwealth" or theocracy was formed in Massachusetts;

- Believed that wealth was sinful;

- Believed in high standards of moral excellence and conscience;

- Believed that birthmarks were signs of sinfulness; and

- Believed in the death penalty for murder, rape, and homosexuality.

To what extent did Captain John Johnson adhere to the beliefs of the Puritan society?

> He boldly said, "There is no room in Christ's army for tolerationists." Johnson was described as one of the earliest and sturdiest in the Puritan pilgrimage. [9]

In regard to some colonists not being made freemen, Johnson said,

> "at the Court in October [1630] many of the first planters were made free; yet afterward none were admitted to this fellowship Churches of Christ; their chiefest aim being bent to promote this work [Church] altogether. The number of freemen this year was about 110." [10]

When the First Church of Newton [now Cambridge] was built in 1632, John Johnson explained that "this year was the first choice of magistrates by freemen; whose number was now increased [by] fifty-three or thereabouts." [11]

Johnson's continued knowledge of religious things was revealed in 1632 about Reverend Mr. Stephen Bachelor when he said, "He was an ancient minister in England; had been a man of fame in his day; was 71 years of age when he came over; brought a number of people with him, and soon became the first feeder of the flock of Christ at Lynn." [12]

Further, John Johnson provided insight into the character of Reverend Mr. Thomas Weld suggesting that Weld:

> "maintained the truth and cleared Christ's Churches here from scandalousreproaches" and about Reverend Mr. Thomas James, "who learned skill to unfold the mind of God in Scripture but continued for some years till some seed of prejudice own by enemies of this work…and removed to New Haven." [13]

Clearly, John Johnson's religious and civic lives were thoroughly intertwined yet well-balanced for the times. John Johnson was surely a creature of the Puritan experiment and his standards influenced the town of Roxbury and its inhabitants in many ways.

It is not written whether John Johnson's Puritan thought was influenced by either of the two clergy from Great Amwell and Ware in England. The Reverend Thomas Hassall of St. John the Baptist Church in Great Amwell was considered a "traditional Anglican" at least during the actual ministry in Great Amwell. He was, though, a rather unconventional preacher, a "hotter sort of Protestant," when preaching at Hoddesdon Chapel to which he was invited as a guest preacher. Hoddesdon is near Great Amwell. There are no significant reasons known for his contradictory religious endeavors in the two sites except, perhaps, for the differing religious requirements of the rural and urban parts of the parish of Great Amwell. Reverend Thomas Hassall was buried in the chancel of the St. Jon the Baptist Church according to the rites of the then banned Book of Common Prayer. This lack act on his behalf may reflect his actual religious leanings toward the Church of England.

On the other hand, Reverend Charles Chauncy, the rector of St. Mary the Virgin Church in Ware where John and Mary Heath Johnson were married in 1613, was always described as a "militant Puritan" who was removed as rector in 1634. To what extent John Johnson attended St. Mary the Virgin Church or was involved with the clergy there is not known.

Religious freedom was not the only reason that the Puritans sought refuge in America. King Charles I, who was King of England and Scotland from 1625-1649, continued to challenge and rebuke the Puritan demands for a more pure Church but also raised taxes on the very people who were well-educated and prosperous. Many of these people happened also to be Puritans. King Charles I failed to realize the growing strength of the merchant/middle class. [14]   "On April 7, 1630, Governor Winthrop, deputy governor Dudley, Sir R. Saltonstall, J. Johnson*, W. Coddington, Charles Fines [Fiennes] esquires, with reverend Mr. George Phillips, on board the Arbella at Yarmouth, sign a humble request of his majesty's loyal subjects the Governor and Company late gone for New England, to rest of their brethren in and of the Church of England, for the obtaining of their prayer, and the removal of suspicions and misconstructions of their intentions [to emigrate to America]. Printed in 4to London, 1630." [15]

[Note: It is not absolutely clear that John Johnson signed this document as stated in the reference or whether it was a misprint for (I)saac Johnson instead of (J)ohn Johnson. The authors believe it was a misprint. John Johnson did not sign this "humble request."]

Regardless, it seems apparent that the leaders of the Winthrop Fleet were very concerned about how the intentions of their emigration to New England might be construed by "brethren in and of the Church of England."   This document was said to be drawn up by that learned, holy, Reverend and famous Mr. White of Dorchester [16]

After the Great Migration from 1629-1640, a Religious Civil War broke out in England. King Charles I was captured and beheaded. Eventually, King Charles' son, Charles II, became King [1660] but not before England experienced a rather austere period of Puritan rule where theaters were closed, literature slumped, and poetry was only seen as good when it talked about God or revealed Holy stories. [17]

Although the Civil War in England restored the Monarchy in 1660, England's religion and politics have never been the same. In fact, the overall influence on young America was a greater freedom in religion and a greater freedom in government than had ever been experienced by any society up to that point.

Religion, as the common thread of motivation in all aspects of Puritan life and emigration itself, has not always been given its rightful place of importance.

Daily life for a Puritan family was from dawn to dusk with all members of the family enduring hardships in many ways. Hardships, though, were thought to be God's test of faithfulness.

Recent scholarship shows that no generalization seems to hold up about the "typical" family life. It is not absolutely certain whether John Johnson and his family were typical. But assuredly every member of the families of the times had a role to play. Everyone worked whether it was candle making, spinning, planting, tending the garden, milking cows, plowing, building, or cooking.

In the Puritan community, the entire "Chosen People" assumed responsibility for fellow Puritans as well as those typed as "Unchosen." The founders of the Massachusetts Bay Colony and the magistrates as well knew the quality of the emigrants because they scrutinized each individual with painstaking care. According to Marcus Lee Hansen, author of The Atlantic Migration (1940), "from the very beginning, their policy was to select from among those who appeared, and this exclusive attitude of New England remained a tradition throughout almost three centuries of immigration. Some arrivals were sent back to England as persons unmeete to inhabit here." [18] Governor Winthrop was authorized to put on a month's notice or probation anyone he thought not fit to "sit down among us without some trial of them." [19] Inhabitancy, or the right to live in a town, was a tremendous issue for the Puritans. By 1631, it was decided by the adoption of a Massachusetts Bay Colony ordinance that the right to vote was confined to those inhabitants who were in "full church communion." [20] Likewise, persons could not legally settle in a town, have land in the Colony, as well as the right of free fishing and hunting without first being voted in as members of the town by the "Selectmen." Further, townspeople could not rent or sell their property without the consent of the town inhabitants. Eventually, town ordinances were passed that allowed a person the right to entertain [lodge] a newcomer for a set period of time. When the period of time was completed and the newcomer was still in the town, a fine was levied against the town person, and the newcomer was given a "warning out" notice. This practice of warning out newcomers continued until 1793. [21]

In November 1635, the following order was passed at a general town meeting of Boston:

> It is agreed that noe further allotments (of land) shallbe graunted unto any new comers, but such as may be likely to be received members of the Congregation; That one shall sell their houses or allotments to any new comers, but with the consent and allowance of those that are appointed Allotters. [22]

In Woburn, Massachusetts, no one was allowed to become an inhabitant without first producing evidence of his "peaceable behavior," and by consent of the selectmen or the town at public meeting.

Roxbury, the town of John Johnson, had an ordinance that stated that no new person should be admitted to any family for more than one week without permission from the selectmen under a penalty of twenty shillings. [23]

On the ninth day of December 1679, the record shows:

> that a warrant was sent to the Constables to take a
> fine of John Jackson for lower (four) weeks
> entertainement of Opertunitie Lane Lane his
> daughter in law Contrary to towne order, and also to
> warne the said Opertunitie to dept the towne or
> giue in securitie to secur the towne from daedg and
> also that if the said Jackson entertaine her longer he
> must expect to pay 3s.4d. p weeke for euery weeke
> after the date hereof. [24]

> *[Note: William Cheney, who emigrated in 1635 to
> Roxbury, Massachusetts, was the father of Elinor
> Cheney who married Humphrey Johnson. He was
> not a Church member until two years before his
> death, but owned land, was a surveyor, and was a
> Selectman in 1656 for Roxbury along with John
> Johnson. William Cheney joined the First Church
> of Roxbury January 5, 1664/5 and was made a
> freeman May 23, 1666. He died June 1, 1667.
> Margaret, his wife, had joined the First Church of
> Roxbury before 1643.]*

Jackson and William Cheney, father-in-law of Humphrey Johnson,
son of Captain John Johnson, secured the town from any damage
that Opertunitie Lane might cause the town.

It was a common Puritan practice to "adopt out" the teenagers of the
family to another chosen family to finish raising them. It was
believed that a different family could provide religious instruction,
in particular, better. It is not known if any of John Johnson's
children lived with other people before emancipation or marriage.
John Johnson did have, however, two granddaughters live in his
household as was stated in his will of 1659. The will does not say
when Elizabeth Johnson, daughter of Isaac Johnson, or Mehitable

Johnson, daughter of Humphrey Johnson lived with John Johnson. At the time of John Johnson's death, Elizabeth Johnson was fourteen years of age and Mehitable Johnson was thirteen years old. Since John Johnson left money in his will for only these two grandchildren, it is possible that they were in his home providing some type or care or services to either him or his wife, Grace Johnson.

Women were clearly the "weaker vessel" in both body and mind. Her husband was instructed by the Puritan minister not only to instruct his wife in religion but [also] to make it easy to [for] her. [25]

It was expected that Puritan husband and wives love each other. It was a duty imposed by God on all married couples. It was a solemn obligation that resulted directly from the marriage contract. If a husband and wife failed to love each other above all the world, they not only wronged each other, they disobeyed God. [26] Marriage was supposed to be a mystic relationship. Not only were the man and wife made of one blood but their union made all the relatives of each of the same blood. [Understanding this belief is important when reading wills of the Seventeenth Century as "relatives" were called "kin," "cousin," "kinsman," "brother," and "sister" interchange-ably.]

A Puritan husband whose wife had died was encouraged to find another for "there would be no marrying in Heaven but [only] a communion of saints." [27]

Only in John Johnson's will do we get an inkling of his affection for Grace Johnson. He called her his "beloved wife" [yet he did not leave her any of his estate saying that he had well taken care of her.]

Marriages were considered valid once consummated by sexual intercourse. A divorce was possible only if a marriage had not been consummated. Puritans practiced rational love rather than romantic love. Love for a wife (or a husband) could not be the same as they had for God. [28] People just did not fall in love but instead entered a "married state." Surprisingly, most of the marriages in Puritan

New England were civil affairs officiated by a magistrate. [29] Puritans believed that nothing in the Bible designated marriage as a religious rite---even pagans got married. [30]

Rite and ceremonies varied from Colony to Colony. The Middle Colonies developed traditions similar to what Americans enjoy today. Emigrants to the Middle Colonies were not so determined to abandon traditional feasts and observances of the Anglican or English Church as were the New Englanders.

The Puritan experience was not democratic in the strictest sense of the word. The authority, thought to be divine, was vested in the magistrates of the Court of Assistants and in the Commonwealth government of New England, and it was necessary to obey them. Governor John Winthrop believed that God had made some rich and some poor, some in high power, and others in mean estate. [31]

John Johnson became a freeman on October 19, 1630 [one record says May 18, 1631]. Because it was a Massachusetts Bay Colony charter requirement that freemen participate in the four-a-year meetings of the Court or Assembly, those who were considered to be a freeman had to be a Puritan and had to provide an oath of allegiance to the government of the Commonwealth of Massachusetts. [32, 33] The designation of "freeman" did not have the meaning that he came "indentured" to someone who paid his way to New England. The designation had the meaning instead that he was a "citizen of the Commonwealth."

John Johnson took his responsibilities for Massachusetts, the town of Roxbury, and his family, quite seriously. A freeman, always in the minority in the Puritan towns, alone voted for the Governor, Magistrates, and the Deputies.

In all aspects of the Puritan community, the minister had the authority to interpret God's plan. He had a special place in the community as the voice of God, and he ministered to the Chosen People, the Puritans. In Roxbury and other New England towns, it was the desire of the Chosen People to understand God's plan since they viewed themselves as God's instruments on earth. The motivation or axis of the Puritan community was the understanding of God's Plan. It was the community, not the individual, which prompted action and decision. John Winthrop made this communal attitude absolutely clear in his speech aboard the *Arbella*, Salem Harbor, 1630 saying, "We must delight in each other, make others' condition our own, rejoice together, mourn together, labor and suffer together, always having before our eyes our community as members of the same body." [34]

Because areas in New England outside of the Massachusetts Bay Colony were developing rapidly, the Puritans had become a minority in its own right and of its own doing. Yet it was the Puritan-conceived laws that greatly influenced the founding of America. The forces that undermined the continuation of the Puritan Society that led to a democracy, were: [35, 36]

- Recognition that people had a natural desire to do right, be moral;

- Dislike of a closed society;

- Lack of democracy; resentment of the powerful few;

- Restrictive environment;

- Growth and changes in their economy;

- Dissention among religious leaders;

- Change from a chartered colony to a Crown [England] colony after the Civil War in England;

- Lack of flexibility;

- Education and becoming more rational about God and the Bible;

- Deaths of John Winthrop and other founders of the Colony;

- Movement westward; mobility of the children of the original Puritan founders; and

- Influence of later immigrants.

There were signs of Puritan Society decay beginning about 1660-1665. The lack of Godliness was increasingly visible in daily and spiritual life. The Puritan pressure to not accumulate wealth and estate gave way to large inventories of personal wealth. John Johnson in 1659 had amassed a sizeable fortune. He was considered one of the wealthiest persons in the Colony at his death. There were subtle changes also even in the family of John Johnson about wealth. Within twelve days after John Johnson's death, his daughter, Mary Johnson Mowry of Providence, Rhode Island, sold her share of the estate of John Johnson. Even within John Johnson's immediate family there was evidence that members did not adhere to all of the teachings of the Puritan movement. In fact, besides Mary Johnson Mowry following the more liberal preacher, Rev. Roger Williams to Providence, RI, Isaac Johnson, son of Captain John Johnson, on January 12, 1642, at the age of twenty-seven, was "admonished to a future time" by the First Church of Roxbury. It is not known just what Isaac Johnson did to deserve censure by the Church authorities. However, it should be pointed out that Isaac Johnson was very active in both Roxbury's civil and military life. Isaac Johnson became a Captain of the Roxbury [Military] Company in 1653 and became the Captain of the Ancient and Honorable Artillery Company in 1665. He was known as a "man of substance and dignity."

Quakers, Anabaptists, and other denominations were beginning to be accepted, and in their own Meeting Houses, the Puritans were subject of violations of the Sabbath such as non-attendance, sleeping during sermons, and swearing.

Mary Johnson Mowry and her husband, Roger, moved to Rhode Island when the Reverend Roger Williams, a friend of Roger Mowry, was banished from the Massachusetts Bay Colony because of his objections to the Biblical interpretations and practices of the

Puritans. So by the 1640's one of the children of John Johnson moved a step closer toward tolerance of other religious denominations.

There was a rise in lawsuits and questions raised about government fairness and honesty. Humphrey Johnson, son of Captain John Johnson, for example, was constantly suing people and the townships regarding land and payments that he believed was due him.

Sins of sex and the use of alcohol were on the increase. And business immorality was noticeable in lying and cheating customers, underpaying workers. Children and grandchildren of the early Puritan founders were brought into the religious beliefs of the Puritans about at the same time as the Church began to lose membership and significance. It was believed that admitting these non-baptized children and grandchildren, the Church would be bolstered and the Puritan influence felt in the communities. But it was not to be.

Overall, the decline of the Puritan Society was inevitable because of the lack of interest in reform toward a more democratic and flexible society as an answer to the rights of the individual. Lastly, the failure of the American Puritans was enhanced when fewer and fewer English Puritans came to America after the return of the English Church to the Crown and the right to worship issue was resolved.

CHAPTER TWO

ADVENTURERS AND THE FORMATION
OF COMPANIES IN ESTABLISHING
NEW ENGLAND

Most history books provide slight reference to Boston Bay settlement efforts prior to the coming of the Puritans in 1630. There were, of course, adventurers to New England prior to 1630. The knowledge in England of the adventurers' attempts to plough the soil, to make homes, and to lay the foundation for the establishment of towns in New England influenced and gave hope to migration. The failure and abandonment of these early efforts to settle America nonetheless provided future emigrants with valuable information to lessen the chances of failure.

In 1614, Captain John Smith explored and mapped New England including Quincy and Weymouth Bays. He called Massachusetts Bay (New England) "the paradise of these parts." [1]

Miles Standish and a party of ten Europeans and three savages in 1621 cast anchor off what is now called Thompson's Island and named it Trevour's Island. [2]

Prior to 1623, Thomas Weston and others tried to establish a fishing industry in New England. It failed. Weston returned to England before April, 1623. Captain Robert Gorges took possession of the buildings left by Weston but by late 1623, even Captain Gorges return to England. Many men and women from the Weston group remained in New England and were still present when the 1630 Winthrop Fleet arrived.

Between 1625-1627, two settlements had been effected in Boston Bay (Nantasket and Squantum). Men who had been ordered to leave the Plymouth Plantation because of charges of civil and spiritual conspiracy, and the intent to disturb the peace established both of these settlements. [3]

Charlestown was established by June 20, 1629 by the Reverends Francis Higginson and Samuel Skelton and several men who had emigrated at their own expense.

Captain Squib anchored the *Mary and John* on May 30, 1630 in Boston Bay near what was Dorchester Heights (now called South Boston). One hundred-twenty people disembarked and had to shift for themselves. [4]

The Dutch, on a colonization scheme which never produced the results they anticipated, explored and settled on the Hudson River in New York and the island of Manhattan in 1626.

Earlier in 1606, King James I chartered two companies -- the Virginia Company of London and the Virginia Company of Plymouth. The Virginia Company of London that settled in the Jamestown area of Virginia was the most aggressive of the two companies. But by 1608, because of the consequence of bickering, exhaustion of supplies, ineffective leadership, the colonists all but abandoned their settlement, Jamestown. Only with continued infusion of support from Company shareholders in England, was the Virginia Company kept alive for a while. [5] It finally failed by 1624.

Failure of the Virginia Company of London left many lessons, however, for future colonizers.

Before the complete failure of the Virginia Company of London, the English Separatists (now called the Pilgrims) developed an agreement with the Virginia Company of London in 1620 to receive land and political self-control in **Virginia.** But, because of a navigational error, they landed and immediately settled in the Cape Cod area of New England. [6]

Abandoned by the English merchant-stockholders because of the

Pilgrims' zeal for religion over that of profit, their economic future was actually secured by the demand for wheat and cattle by the large Winthrop migration (Massachusetts Bay Company) in 1630 to the Massachusetts Bay Colony.

The Massachusetts Bay Company was originally the New England Company (1629). Because of problems of title to the land and governance, the Charter by King Charles I was re-issued as the Massachusetts Bay Company to Sir Richard Saltonstall, Isaac Johnson, Hugh Peter, John Winthrop and others. Not having named (perhaps intentionally or not) a Company Headquarters (likely London, England) in the Charter, the Massachusetts Bay Company was free to establish the Colony with its own concept of government and religion without interference from the Monarchy or the Church of England. [7]

So they came in "companies." While it is widely known that Puritan leaders and their relatives, friends, and relatives of friends settled New England in the 1630's, we only recently have begun to understand that they called themselves "companies" and how they were formed in England. The Winthrop Fleet, headed by John Winthrop, was surely an example of a "Gentlemen's Company." Once he had committed himself to the Massachusetts enterprise, he scoured the areas known best to him, around the family base in Groton in southwestern Suffolk, and also in northeastern Essex, around Great Stambridge, where he had married his first wife. Winthrop was instrumental in hiring the ships that would carry the passengers in 1630, in providing provisions for these passengers, and in seeing to it that the passenger lists included the practitioners of such useful trades as carpentry and blacksmithing. [8] He also looked for men with military experience to help in the defense of the new colony. It is the belief of the author that John Winthrop recruited John Johnson. In some cases, families migrated together. When whole emigrant families and their extended relatives did not migrate together, there is strong evidence that the extended families followed their emigrant relatives within the next few years.

Three distinct types of leaders usually recruited these companies, most all with the common thread of Puritan leanings. For example, John Winthrop's fleet of ships was organized well in advance by Winthrop, Isaac Johnson and other gentlemen as well as many of Lady Arbella Johnson's Earl of Lincolnshire relatives and clients. There is no doubt that Winthrop had made by his mind for New England by the summer of 1629. [9]

Winthrop was a planner and a writer. He drafted at least five copies of his "Particular Considerations" and "General Conclusions" both that set forth the main principles for emigration. He most privately shared these documents in Puritan strongholds of Sempringham, London, Bury St. Edmunds, and Cambridge with likeminded men and relatives. [10]

It is recognized now how important the extended family connections were to the survival of the emigrants. The emigrants, of course, established themselves in various towns based upon their previous association in England.

The 1630 Lincolnshire Company, more commonly called the Massachusetts Bay Company or the *Winthrop Fleet of 1630*, was highly organized, and much effort was exerted to have a balance of professions and trades so that the Massachusetts Bay Colony could be self-sufficient. Craftsmen, tradesmen, farmers, lawyers, civic leaders, preachers, and a physician were a few of those among the Winthrop Fleet. The timing of the departure from England provided the emigrants with ample time to build houses and prepare for the winter.

Some historians believe that because only two preachers came in 1630, namely Rev. John Wilson and Rev. George Phillips, the intent of the Lincolnshire company was to form only one town instead of the seven or eight established in the Colony.

Puritan ministers commonly called a "Cleric Company" led another form of a New England-bound company. Because the English authorities complained that the Puritan lay people "were subversively prone to gadding to sermons," about the only alternative was to migrate to New England so they could continue their zeal of sermonizing. It is said that many local priests in the Church of England just could not satisfy the exacting standard set forth by the Puritans. [11]

The awe-inspiring influential preachers convinced their parishioners to join the companies for the purpose of emigration to New England. According to Professor Roger Thompson of East Anglia University, "Six hundred sixty-seven emigrants can be counted in the various 'religious companies' that followed persecuted ministers across the Atlantic." [12]

Companionship between family members as well as between people of a Puritan commonality provided the sense of belonging and worth to those who traded English soil for that of New England.

Extraordinary and powerful as Church membership and gentry class leadership were to the formation of companies, the greatest common connection was between family and extended family members. It is not believed that John Johnson came to New England with brothers or sisters but he did bring his children by his first wife, Mary Heath Johnson, and a new 2nd wife, Margery _____. At least three sources, however, have speculated that Isaac Johnson, one of the leaders and financiers of the Winthrop Fleet, was a kinsman [perhaps a cousin] to John Johnson.

Isaac Johnson was baptized in 1601 in Stamford, Lincolnshire, England. He was the son of Abraham and Anne Meadows Johnson. He married Lady Arbella Fiennes on April 5, 1623. Lady Arbella was the daughter of Thomas, third Earl of Lincoln. Lady Arbella Johnson died in Salem, Massachusetts in August 1630 and Isaac Johnson died September 30, 1630 presumably in Boston, Massachusetts. Isaac Johnson's grandfather was Archdeacon Robert Johnson, a staunch Puritan who established Oakham and Uppingham Hospitals and Schools. Isaac Johnson's great-grandfather was gentleman Maurice Johnson, of Stamford, England. [Johnson of Clipsham and Pinchbeck] [13]

Professor Thompson believes that the successful yet "staggering" achievement of transporting thirteen to twenty thousand English people to New England within a decade," is supported by the notion that family connections bolstered the weak and scared. Further, he cites that "family" provided community and continuity, in addition to fostering the advantage of pooled resources of skills and knowledge.[14]

The persistence of family and extended family supported the network of inter-reliance that was basic and absolute to the successful establishment of towns and culture in New England.

CHAPTER THREE

JOHN JOHNSON'S MOTIVATION
TO MIGRATE TO AMERICA

Without personal materials, letters or statements made by John Johnson about why he chose to uproot his family, leave his home country and relatives, it becomes somewhat educated guesswork what his motives were to migrate to America.

Professor Roger Thompson, East Anglia University, pointed out in an e-mail message to the author that motivation was usually a mixture of motives. Religion, as previously cited in this book, provided a singular reason for John Johnson to join with other Puritans in the 1630 Winthrop Fleet. [1] However, as Thompson suggested, John Johnson may have been equally motivated by the promise of land and hope for economic betterment.

Winthrop, Governor of the Massachusetts Bay Colony, wrote in 1629 "that we are grown to that height of Intemperance in all excess of Riot, as no man's estate [in England] almost will suffice to keep sail with his equals: and he that fails in it must live in scorn and contempt." [2]

English Yeomen, like John Johnson, may have been caught in the bind of dealing with middlemen in the selling of his excess crops over and above his family's need for subsistence. Furthermore, perhaps John Johnson did not own land but merely rented acres of farmland from the Gentry. Renting would further reduce any possible profit.

Virginia D. Anderson, in New England's Generation says, "still other scholars have argued more recently that a combination of religious, economic, social and political factors informed individual decisions to move, and that these tangled strands defy unraveling." [3]

Norman C.P. Tyack, however, in his 1951 University of London doctoral dissertation "Migration from East Anglia to New England Before 1660" maintained that religion may well have encouraged the emigration of "humbler folk." He did, though, provide substantial insight into other significant factors that motivated migration to New England. These were: (1) the effect on the English population by reoccurring plagues between 1620 and 1640, and (2) the economic conditions for the middle and lower classes.

Serious outbreaks of illness in 1625 and 1627 bringing death to no less than 1431 people in the three counties (Essex, Norfolk, and Suffolk) identified in the Tyack dissertation as "East Anglia." People were so devastated by these plagues that they had no means to live by. Everything was restricted or stopped: work, transportation, communication, trade, and travel. At the same time, the Royal government levied special rates or taxes for the relief of the stricken thus resulting in a heavy burden for many. [4]

As early as 1618, King James I strictly and rigidly controlled the lands that lay outside the vast Royal Forest. The political struggle for more land by English yeomen, husbandmen, and even laborers, resulted in great uncertainty in England. There was hope with the promise of free land in New England. These desperate Puritans and non-Puritans had nothing to lose but everything to gain in a new existence in the New England Commonwealth. [5]

Further complicating the economic conditions in England in the period 1620-1640, was the lack of sophistication of appropriate marketing strategies of products grown or made such as corn, barley, rye, wheat, beans, peas, hides, wool, malt, and textiles.

It is without question that John Johnson, as a yeoman (farmer) was affected by the economic problems of England, and perhaps motivated to immigrate to New England.

There was a migration of sorts within England about the same time as Puritans were packing up for the voyage across the Atlantic Ocean. Comparing the two "migrations," it is found that in England the migration was by the young and poor who were bound for a better life in the cities of England. In contrast, the Puritans were not particularly young. In fact, many were about forty [the average age was 37 for men], the same age as John Johnson. The Puritans were clearly not going to New England to the cities for a better life. There were none. Further, many Puritans were middle class and higher from social and economic standpoints.

Any study of migration cannot be valid without recognition that migration offered an escape from conditions unfavorable in local, rural communities in England.

In England, in the early Seventeenth Century, farmers or yeomen, outnumbered craftsmen by seven to one. Most yeomen farmed about 50 acres of land. Besides providing for the family, a farm of 50 acres might be productive enough to sell enough on the market to allow relative prosperity.

Doctor Anderson indicates that the cost of emigration was about 25 Pounds, which was the same as the annual rent for a 50-acre plot of land in England in the 1630s. [6]

The irony of the suggestion that the Puritans emigrated for the opportunity of land and betterment is haunting. On the one hand, Puritans were constantly reminded that they had "misplaced their affections through greed and extravagant apparel that was leading to the erosion of personal piety. [7] On the other hand, the lower and middle class were striving to have a better life that wealth in New England could not provide.

The guilt placed upon the Puritans was tremendous. Thomas Dudley, an early leader and later a Governor, warned that anyone who sailed for material gain "comits an errour of which he will soon repent him." [8] Reverend Eleazar Mather threatened the "Hell into" the Puritans by asserting that, "when the abounding of temporal blessings is accompanied with the abounding of sin, the Lord was preparing to abandon his wayward people. [9]

John Johnson did not seem to be threatened (by God) nor chastised (by fellow Puritans) for his above-average land holdings, carpeted house, fine clothing, and accumulation of comfortable worldly goods.

What then, motivated John Johnson to immigrate to New England? What provided him with the courage and confidence? What affected John Johnson's attitudes and values?

Thompson, in <u>Mobility and Migration</u>, likely says it best about the migration of Puritans to New England in the 1600s.

Yeoman John Johnson, first of all, may have had an education away from his hometown. We believe that he was in London at the Honourable Artillery Company by 1612, so he had some experience traveling from his hometown to London. Secondly, upon marrying Mary Heath in Ware, England in 1613, it is probable that John Johnson had the experience of traveling from one village to another as well as settling in a town other than one in which he grew up. Having his children by Mary Heath Johnson baptized in both Ware and in Great Amwell might mean that he moved at least once or twice between 1613 and 1630. John Johnson's farming may have led him by barges and carts to markets away from Ware and Great Amwell. [10]

At age forty or so, he had confidences from these mobility experiences thus was unafraid to move to New England.

Coupled with these confidences, he more than likely felt it was safe to travel to New England because his friends and fellow Puritans were also making the voyage.

In the third place, if John Johnson was only a renter instead of a landowner, he might have been motivated by the possibility of land. By 1640, for example, Governor John Winthrop and his wife, had land grants totaling more than 5,000 acres. John Johnson, himself, was granted hundreds of acres for services rendered to the Massachusetts Bay Colony. Some of the land was sold to other [for profit] and yet other acreage was given to family members.

In terms of religion, it is well documented that John Johnson was an extraordinary Puritan, and as such was probably unhappy with England and the treatment toward the Puritans.

Lastly, the fact that John Johnson was so active and so competent in civil and religious affairs in Roxbury and the Massachusetts Bay Colony, suggests that he might have had similar experiences prior to emigration. Perhaps knowledge of the probable administrative structure of the Colony before emigration, may have been a factor in influencing John Johnson to sail to New England.

The ingredients for John Johnson's motivation to migrate were probably mixed just like nearly all the other Puritan emigrants in the 1600s.

Even without the specifics, it would seem that once we know who John Johnson is, we begin to understand why he came in the Winthrop Fleet.

CHAPTER FOUR

THE WINTHROP FLEET

John Johnson, his wife Margery, and six children by his first wife, Mary Heath Johnson, left London in the ship *Arbella* on April 6, 1630 and were among 80 families in the Winthrop Fleet. The *Arbella*, the lead ship, was named in honor of Lady Arbella Johnson who was the wife of Isaac Johnson. Isaac Johnson, considered to be one of the wealthiest emigrants, was instrumental in planning a company for the voyage with their families, friends, and personal property to establish a plantation in New England for permanent settlement.

John Winthrop and other members of the organizing Colonists kept the voyage to New England as secret as possible for fear of retaliation from the Monarchy and other officials. But clearly, discussions took place as early as 1628. [1]

The founders of the Massachusetts Bay Colony were dominated by a group of conservative merchants, lawyers, clergy, and manufacturers under the leadership of Matthew Craddock. Without their financial support, the *Arbella* and its companion ships in the Winthrop Fleet would never have sailed. [2]

The success of the Winthrop Fleet colonization of Massachusetts Bay probably is a result of having two years or more to plan the formation of the company. This company of emigrants included in addition to professional people, tradesmen and men who were experienced in governance. The Massachusetts Bay Colony Company was successful where earlier companies from England had failed.

While John Winthrop had an extraordinary and overwhelming financial motivation to emigrate and was a "late recruit," he was apprehensive as to the future of England in addition to his own fortunes. He wrote to his wife Margaret (Tyndal) in May 1629, "I am verilye persuaded God will bring some heavy affliction upon this lande [England] and that speedylie." [3] Further, distraught over finances, Winthrop explained to his wife, "Where we shall spend the rest of our short tyme I knowe not: the Lorde, I trust, will direct us in mercye." [4]

During the voyage and up to his death in 1649, John Winthrop habitually interpreted events as providences of God, the causer of things. [5]

In the voyage across the Atlantic Ocean from England to Massachusetts Bay, the Winthrop Fleet were named as follows: [6]

Ship	Designation
Arbella	- 'Admiral'
Talbot	- 'Vice-Admiral'
Ambrose	- 'Rear-Admiral'
Jewel	- 'Captain'

It is not known whether the "nautical designations" had anything to do with class distinctions as determined by Governor Winthrop and the English Society, or the naming the ships merely provided the order in which they would cross the Atlantic.

All of the above-named ships carried passengers while the rest of the Winthrop Fleet ships were used to transport personal belongings of the passengers, plants and roots, seed, supplies, and live stock.

A fee of 5 Sterling Pounds was charged per adult person to cover the cost of meals, which included the availability of beer.   [The amount of beer was over 10,000 gallons for the trip.]   Children's fees were less than the adult fare, and children who were still breast-feeding were not charged at all.   Additional charges were approximately 4 Sterling Pounds for a ton of freight and livestock.

A family the size of John Johnson's would have a total fee of over 30 Sterling Pounds, which would be about $2,000 in United States Dollars in 1999.

The organizers of the Winthrop Fleet were very specific about what items and goods emigrants should bring to New England. The listing below is suggested for "one person which being doubled may serve for as many as you please." [7]

Victuals for a whole year for a Man, and so After the rate for more:

8 bushes of meal
2 bushes of pease
2 bushes of oatmeal
1 gallon of aua-vitae
1 gallon of oil
2 gallons of vinegar
1 firkin of butter

Apparel

1 Monmouth cap
3 falling bands
3 shirts
1 waistcoat
1 suit of canvass
1 suit of cloth
3 pair of stockings
4 pair of shoes
2 pair of sheets
7 ells of canvass, to make a bed and bolster

1 pair of blankets
1 coarse rug

Arms

1 armour, complete
1 long piece
1 sword
1 belt
1 bandoleer
20 pound of powder
60 pound of lead
1 pistol and goose shot

Tools

1 broad hoe
1 narrow hoe
1 broad axe
1 felling axe
1 steel handsaw
1 hammer
1 shovel
1 spade
2 augers
4 chisels
2 piercers, stocked
1 gimlet
1 hatchet
2 frowers (edged tool)
1 handbill (edged tool with a hook)

1 grindstone
1 pickaxe
Nails of all sorts

Household Implements

1 iron pot
1 kettle
1 frying pan
1 gridiron
2 skillets
1 spit
Wooden platters
Dishes
Spoons
Trenchers

Spices

Sugar
Pepper
Cloves
Mace
Cinnamon
Nutmegs, fruit

Also, there are divers [sundry] other things necessary to be taken over to this Plantation, as books, nets, hooks and lines, cheese, bacon, kine, goats &c.

We know, of course, that farm animals, wagons, and household furniture was brought to the Massachusetts Bay Colony in the Winthrop Fleet.

By June 12, 1630, the *Arbella* anchored in the Massachusetts Bay in the area of Salem, Massachusetts and by July 6, 1630, with the arrival of the *Success*, a freight ship, all of the ships of the Winthrop Fleet had arrived in New England.

John Johnson was in the lead ship, the *Arbella*, with Governor John Winthrop and other leaders of the Company. He was the quartermaster for the trip.

The names and ages upon arrival of the Johnson family who immigrated to America in 1630 are:

Name	Age Upon Arrival
John, husband	about 40 years of age
Margery, 2nd wife	about 35-40 years of age

(children by Mary Heath, 1st wife)

Mary, daughter	16 years of age
Isaac, son	15 years of age
Elizabeth, daughter	11 years of age
Humphrey, son	10 years of age
Sarah, daughter	5 years of age
Hannah, daughter	3 years of age

Charles E. Banks, author of The Winthrop Fleet, remarkably was able to reconstruct most of the passenger list of the Winthrop Fleet.

Among the 1630 passengers who settled in Roxbury, Massachusetts along with John Johnson were: [8]

Alcock, George	Goldthwaite, Thomas
Alcock, _____	Goldthwaite, Elizabeth
Baxter, Gregory	Johnson, John
Burr, Jehu	Johnson, Margery
Burr, _____	Johnson, Mary
Burr, Jesu (son)	Johnson, Isaac
Chase, William	Johnson, Elizabeth
Cole, Robert	Johnson, Humphrey
Crafts, Griffin	Johnson, Sarah
Crafts, Alice	Johnson, Hannah
Crafts, Hannah (daughter)	Lamb, Thomas (senior)
Lamb, Elizabeth	Pratt, Abraham
Lamb, Thomas (junior)	Pratt, Jane
Lamb, John	Rawlins, Thomas (senior)
Lamb, Samuel	Rawlins, Mary
Porter, John	Rawlins, Thomas (junior)
Porter, Margaret	Rawlins, Nathaniel
Porter, _____	Rawlins, John
Porter, _____	Rawlins, Joan
Porter, _____	Rawlins, Mary
Porter, _____	Smythe, Francis
Smythe, _____ (probably a wife)	

In the Banks' Winthrop Fleet of 1630 book, the account of some passengers lacks town designations for scores of emigrants. A more scholarly and dependable account of New England arrivals is The Great Migration Begins by Robert Charles Anderson that is published by the New England Historic Genealogical Society (1995).

CHAPTER FIVE

TOWNS AND VILLAGES WHERE
JOHN JOHNSON LIVED

English records of land transactions, leasing, taxation, and other types of records have not provided concrete evidence of John Johnson's place of birth or where his parents might have lived.

Birth and baptismal records of the children of John and Mary Heath Johnson have been most reliable for the English information about John Johnson. After 1630, the Massachusetts Bay Colony records are clear that John Johnson and his second wife, Margery, lived in Roxbury, Massachusetts, a distance of two to three miles from Boston, Massachusetts at the time of formation.

Ware, England

John Johnson was in Ware, England at least by 1613 as he married Mary Heath on September 21, 1613. Roger Thompson, author of Mobility and Migration, suggests that in his study of nearly 2000 English emigrants from "East Anglia", more than fifty per cent of them married within four miles of their own birthplace if the place of marriage was not already the male's birthplace.

The first child (Mary) of John Johnson was baptized in Ware, England in 1614 so an assumption can be made that John and Mary Heath Johnson lived in Ware and/or Ware End.

> *[Note: The next six children were baptized in Great Amwell, England making the author believe that the Johnsons physically moved to Great Amwell from Ware. On the other hand, Ware End was actually*

39

part of Great Amwell "at the End near Ware." Ware
End was a heavily populated, poor quarter of the
Ware township. It is possible that the Johnsons
never moved but were listed in parishes of Great
Amwell and Ware at a later date by historians.]

The next two children, Sarah and Joseph, were baptized in Ware. Hannah, the tenth child is not listed in either Ware or Great Amwell records.

It is believed that Ware [from early Waras] was settled about 894 A.D. when "pagans brought their ships up the Thames River and after that, up the Lige (Lea) River and began to throw up their fortifications near the river at the distance of 20 miles from London." [1]

Traditionally, however, it is held that the founding of Ware was by Edward, the Elder, King Alfred's son, in 914 A.D.

Roughly between 900 and 1100, early Ware was a malting center of barley, which was then dispatched to London on barges down the River Lea.

In 1078 there was evidence of a Church or Benedictine Priory. [2]

The Lea [Lee] River has played an important role in the prosperity of Ware. At the time John Johnson lived and farmed in Ware, the river was used to transport grain such as corn, barley, and wheat to London.

By the time John Johnson left Ware and Great Amwell, the Lea River had been repaired several times by the removal of shelves and shoals in the river.

In 1571, the Lea River was the subject of great concern of the citizens of London and of the Country [England], so much so that it resulted in the following Act of Parliament: [3]

"Act for bringing the Rover of the Lee to the North Side of the Citie of London,"

"For as much as is perceived by many grave and wise men, as well of the Citie of London as of the country, that it were Very commodious and profitable, both for the Citie and the countrythat the River of the Lee [Lea] otherwise called 'Ware River', might be brought within the land to the North part of the said Citie of London, the same to be cut out of the said river in the Most aptest and meetest places of the said river Lee, to convey From thence the leading and the passage of the said water Through such a convenient and meet cut as may be secure for the navigation of barges and other vessels, and for the carriage And conveying, as well of merchandise, corn, and victuals, as Other necessaries, from the Town of Ware unto the said Citie Of London, and from the said Citie to the said places and the Towne of Ware. And also for the Tiltbotes, and Wherries, for Conveying of the Queen's subjects to and fro, so their great Ease and commoditie."

[Note: This endeavor cost the City of London 80,000 Pounds, a very large sum in the Seventeenth Century.]

From very early times a footpath, and later a highway, wound along the west side of Lea Valley near Ware by the forest to London. A Roman military road replaced the old footpath and by 900 A.D. the Roman Road from Ware to London was called Ermine Street.

In 1623, a time when John Johnson still lived in the area, the state of the roads was deplorable. Shortly after John Johnson left for America in 1630, the roads in and around Ware were "given a rest: by order of King Charles I." That is, all wheeled traffic, packhorses, and any two-wheeled carts with more than five horses were banned.

The highways and roads were eventually repaired by 1672.

Because of the beauty of the rolling hills in the area of Ware, and the fact that Ware was on a major highway [to Cambridge and farther north to Scotland] many Inns, Taverns, Ale Houses, and Manor Houses existed for the pleasure of the travelers.

> *[Note: An interesting note is that Ware, in 1618, was one of the three towns in the county of Hertfordshire to store munitions. John Johnson of Roxbury, Massachusetts was solely in charge of the munitions for the Massachusetts Bay Colony. One wonders whether there is a connection.]*

There was a Ware Free School by 1612. The schoolhouse was a wooden building and stood in the corner of the Churchyard (St. Mary the Virgin.) [4]

Great Amwell, England

Great Amwell, England is a very, very small village located on the right bank of the Lea River across from Ware. Great Amwell is nineteen miles north of London and one and half miles from the center of Ware.

The Lea River was channeled into two rivers, and the "new river" conveyed fresh water to London via wooden pipes and pumps. The new river channel runs immediately along- side St. John the Baptist Church where many of the children of John and Mary Heath Johnson were baptized.

The main focal point of Great Amwell is the Church. Currently, the parish boundaries are approximately four miles by two and a half miles covering two thousand-five hundred acres, slightly smaller than in the time of John Johnson. Only 244 acres were suitable for farming. With so little acreage available, it raises the question whether John Johnson actually lived in Great Amwell and farmed acreage in both Great Amwell and Ware, or lived in Ware and farmed in both villages.

If John Johnson lived in Great Amwell at the time of the baptisms of some of his children (1615-1623), there were no more than 120 houses.

While the font used for baptisms at the St. John the Baptist Church in Great Amwell is modern, the oak communion table is the same one used in the 17th Century when John and Mary Heath Johnson worshipped in the Church. Furthermore, the communion plate dates to 1620.

Great Amwell's "claim to fame" was its position along two major routes leading to London: the Lea River and the Old North Road. Great Amwell, which had limited acreage for growing corn and barley, was primarily a poor farming village. While Ware became the inland port for barges and other river traffic, Great Amwell could barely muster Inns and Taverns to accommodate travelers along the Old North Road. During the time of John Johnson, Great Amwell did have a fishery in the mill pond on the Lea River. [6]

Because of its perceived healthfulness, Great Amwell became a haven for nurse-children who were provided mainly from London. However, in John Johnson's time, at least one burial in ten was a non-resident nurse-child. Providing nursing (breast feeding) to London's children was considered a "cottage industry." [7]

There was much mobility of the Great Amwell residents in the fifty-seven years Thomas Hassell, Vicar of St. John the Baptist, served Great Amwell and recorded the Parish Register. Less than twenty-five per cent of the first entries in his book remain at its ending. [8]

By May 15, 1629, the wife of John Johnson, Mary Heath Johnson, had died, and John Johnson left for America by April 6, 1630.

Roxbury, Massachusetts

The first settlement of Roxbury was in 1630 shortly after the arrival of the *Winthrop Fleet*.   Roxbury was settled by people from northwestern Essex, southwestern Suffolk, and the neighboring towns of eastern Hertfordshire. [9]   Roxbury first appeared as "Rocbury" and "Rocksborough" in early Massachusetts Bay records. Some early settlers, however, called Roxbury "Muddy River" because of its proximity to the river.   Charles M. Ellis, in The History of Roxbury Town, believes that there might have been evidence of huts or clearings of prior [native] habitation but the Roxbury of the Puritans was begun in June or July 1630. [10]   John Johnson was one of the founders of Roxbury and lived his entire life there.

It has been remarked that, "the Roxbury people were of the best that came." [11] In describing the people of Roxbury, Albert B. Hart said, "the inhabitants of it being all very rich. Roxbury had good ground for corn, and meadows for cattle." [12]   Mr. H.A.S. Dearborn in an address of the Second Centennial Anniversary of the Settlement of Roxbury, said, "(D)uring the long period of the colonial government, the citizens of Roxbury were conspicuous for their patriotism and liberality; they were ever ready to afford their aid in all measures which were deemed important to the general weal." [13] [commonwealth.]

For the first two years, the small group of Roxbury Puritans attended Church [Meeting House] at Dorchester, approximately a mile away through the forest, until the First Church of Roxbury was built in 1632.

A "free schoole" was erected prior to 1645. John Johnson, one of its founders, joined with Reverend John Eliot and at least sixty families of Roxbury to establish the school. The significance of the Roxbury Latin School, as it was called, was that it was conceived by the citizens of Roxbury, supported by the whole town, and relied upon the generosity of the townspeople for land, money, and labor. For more than 250 years, the "free schoole" was not supported or aided by public funds.

John Johnson was active in many civic activities in Roxbury that are covered in that chapter. The paramount importance of education, both military and civil, had taken possession of the minds of the founders including John Johnson. The "free schoole" had immense force of culture to the mass of American citizenship, and may have contributed as much as anything to the unparalleled intellectual and moral influence in Massachusetts. [14]

John Johnson lived near Pritchard Island that was adjacent to a marsh at the mouth of Stony River. John Johnson's son-in-law [Robert Pepper] had property just west of John Johnson's on Stony River.

The account of John Johnson in the History of Roxbury Town by Ellis, says:

> John Johnson, freeman in 1631. He was generally in public life. He represented this town in the first general court, and for fourteen years afterwards. He was a military man also, and was appoynted surveyor generall of all ye armes. The public stores were placed in his house, and it was when that was burnt and blown up that the town records were destroyed. He died September 29, 1659, leaving L 660. He kept a tavern. Many public meetings

were held at Brother Johnson's.

Roxbury was described as "a fair and handsome country town, the inhabitants of it being all very rich." [15]

In a document called "A Note of the Estates and Persons of the Inhabitants of Rocksbury, 1636-1640," John Johnson was one of the most wealthy of the sixty-nine heads of households. His estate was valued at 15 Pounds, 12 Shillings. Only those of the Gentry class were slightly wealthier. [16]

Ellis says that Roxbury had a great number of very opulent citizens. In 1654, the town is described:

> "situated between Boston and Dorchester, being well watered with coole and pleasant Springs issuing forth [from] the Rocky-hills, and with small Freshets, watering theVallies of this fertill Towne, whose forme is somewhat like a wedge double pointed, entering between the two foure named Townes, filled with a laborious people, who labours the Lord hath so blest, that, in the roome of dismall swamps and tearing bushes, they hae very goodly Fruit-trees, fruitfull fields and gardens, their Heard of Cows, Oxen and other young Cattell of that kind about 350 and dwelling houses near upon 120. Their Streetes are large, and some fayre howses, yet have they built their Howse for Church-assembly destitute and unbeautified with other buildings. The church of Christ is here increased to about 120 persons." [17]

John Johnson was always a farmer and tavern owner but he fully participated in Massachusetts Bay Colony affairs, civic and Church issues of Roxbury, and defended Roxbury and the Colony against the Indians.

CHAPTER SIX

THE MARRIAGES OF JOHN JOHNSON

Only in the last decade has the first marriage of John Johnson been verified from records in the Hertfordshire Record Office in Hertford, England.

John Johnson was married three times.   Some accounts of his marriages, based upon usually reliable sources as well as from competent genealogists, only credit him with two marriages: **Margery** _____, listed as wife number one, and **Grace Negus Fawer** as wife number two. However, there were **three** marriages with the first being **Mary Heath**.

Mary Heath was born to William Heath of Ware, Hertfordshire, England and Agnes Cheney Heath of Waltham Abbey, Essex, England.   Mary Heath was baptized on March 24, 1593/4 at St. Mary the Virgin Church, in Ware, England.[1] William Heath, father of Mary Heath, was born by 1570, son of Edward Heath and Alice

_____.

Agnes Cheney was the fourth child of Robert Cheney and Joan Harrison Cheney. It has been suggested that Agnes Cheney was born about 1560 in Waltham Abbey, Essex, England. [2,3]
.

Mary Heath married John Johnson, September 21, 1613 at the St. Mary the Virgin Church in Ware, England. Mary Heath Johnson died *before* John Johnson immigrated to America in 1630 and was buried May 15, 1629, in the cemetery surrounding St. Mary the Virgin Church in Ware.   John Johnson and Mary Heath Johnson had ten children. These children are discussed in the "Churches of John Johnson," Chapter Seven, as well as the "Genealogy of John Johnson," Chapter Nine.

John Johnson's second marriage was to a Margery _____. In order to sort out just who "Margery" might be, the author explored the eight small villages in addition to Roxbury and Boston that were started by the Puritans of the Massachusetts Bay Colony prior to 1635. The villages were: Watertown, Dorchester, Medford, Saugus, Charleston, Concord, Dedham, and Sudbury. The reason for a survey of the marriages in these particular villages is because of references made that "Margery Johnson" probably married him (John) about 1633. One of the suggestions made by author Douglas Richardson in the New England Historic and Genealogical Register CXVVI, July, 1992, was that "Margery _____, 2nd wife of John Johnson, probably married him about 1633 inasmuch as she was number 90 on the First Church of Roxbury rolls provided by Reverend John Eliot. [4] However, in the 1908 book, History of the First Church in Roxbury by Walter Eliot Thwing, Margery Johnson is listed as a Founder of the First Church in Roxbury, which was established prior to 1633. [5] Further, joining the Church in Colonial times depended upon the person being ready to be admitted. There are too many examples of colonists who joined the Church well after their arrival in Massachusetts Bay for anyone to form strong conclusions about a marriage between John Johnson and Margery _____ taking place in New England.

In search of the surname of Margery, the author researched the marriage records in the Massachusetts Vital Records for Roxbury to 1850, the records of the First Church of Roxbury, the references in the History of Roxbury, as well as the somewhat reliable New England Marriages Prior to 1700 by Clarence A. Torrey with corrections and additions by Melinde Lutz Sanborn.

Unfortunately, none of the above resources made any reference to a marriage of Margery _____ and John Johnson. In a list of Roxbury Church members from the Rev. John Eliot's Record provided in the Memorials of the Pilgrim Fathers (John Eliot and His Friends of Nazing and Waltham Abbey) by W. Winters, F. R. Historical Society, John Johnson is listed with his wife, Margery. Unfortunately, this book was published in 1882 from "original sources" but the sources are not dated.

John Johnson's third marriage was to Grace Negus Fawer of Dorchester, Massachusetts.[6] Grace Negus came to America on May 27, 1634 along with her brother, Jonathan Negus. In some early records, "Negus" was sometimes spelled "Negoose and Negoos."

Grace Negus was baptized in England, possibly Shelton, county of Bedford, on January 5, 1603. She married John Johnson, her second husband, before October 14, 1656. Grace Negus became a member of the First Church, Boston, on July 27, 1634. Her Will, dated December 21, 1671 and proved in Suffolk County, Massachusetts on February 14, 1671 appointed her brother Jonathan Negus as executor and divided all of her estate between her brothers Jonathan and Benjamin Negus.

Prior to the marriage of Grace Negus Fawer to John Johnson, Grace Negus was married to Barnabas Fawer as his second wife. Fawer and Grace Negus Fawer had one child, Abigail who was baptized July 30, 1644 in Dorchester, Massachusetts. It is suggested in The Ancestry of Emily Jane Angell written by Dean Crawford Smith and edited by Melinde Lutz Sanborn that Abigail Fawer died prior to her father and before her mother, Grace Negus Fawer, married John Johnson.[7] Grace Fawer Johnson did not have any children by John Johnson of Roxbury.

Many professional and amateur genealogists, unfortunately, continue the myth that John Johnson was married second (and sometimes, first) to Margery Scudder. Margery Scudder was NOT ever married to John Johnson. Some genealogies **erroneously** list children of Mary Heath Johnson and John Johnson as born to Margery Scudder. The author has seen references to Margery Scudder and John Johnson dated as early as 1900. The Margery Scudder connection was based upon the Will of William Scudder of Darenth, England in which he gave money to a John Johnson, the elder, and a John Johnson, the younger.

William and Margaret Scudder did have a daughter named Margaret (Margery).

Mr. Simon Skudder of Bristol, England, in 1998 provided the author with substantial Scudder-Skudder family information in England and the Scudders in America.

Following the Pepper Genealogy references to "Scudder" as Margery's surname, D. L. Jacobus and W.H. Wood, in the journal American Antiquarian Society, Vol. VII, published in 1943, provided continued confusion about a Margery Scudder by indicating that Margery Scudder was a daughter of William Scudder of Darenth, Kent, England, and was the wife of John Johnson. Further, the article also stated that John Johnson was a native of Herne (Herne Hill), Kent, England where his family had "resided for more than a generation." [8]

> [Note: The Genealogy of Captain John Johnson of Roxbury, Mass. by Paul Franklin Johnson, 1951, established with assistance from Ada Modern Johnson's research, that "John Johnson was from 12 miles north of London where many of his relatives still live."] [9]

The 1626 Will of Margery Scudder, William Scudder's widow, then of Newington Butts, Surrey, plus intervening Kent marriage records for two of his daughters, Joane and Margaret, however, raise SERIOUS doubts that **ANY** of the Scudder daughters is the "Margery" who married John Johnson. In Margery Scudder's will of 1626, only the name of her youngest daughter, Mary (by then, Freeman) is specifically mentioned, and that being executrix. The older daughters, including Margaret/Margery are presumed deceased. Margery also leaves bequests to William Chapman, her grandson, and to Mary Stacey, her granddaughter by Margaret Scudder Stacey and Thomas Stacey.

Margery Scudder, widow of William Scudder, also leaves brass pots to Thomas Stacey, but nothing to any Margaret or Margery Scudder nor any Margaret or Margery Stacey. [10]

Margaret (Margery) Scudder married Thomas Stacey of Westerham, Kent, England in 1610.

Margery Scudder Stacey, the "Margery" who allegedly married John Johnson, was not living by 1626. John Johnson's first wife died in 1629. Therefore, the authors has concluded that it would have been impossible for Margery Scudder, who actually would have been Margery Scudder Stacey, to have married John Johnson between 1629 and 1635. In fact, on the basis of the mounting evidence, it seems absolutely unlikely that Margery_____, wife of John Johnson, *was ever* a daughter of William Scudder of Darenth, or even a Scudder at all.

Furthermore, there is no evidence that the John Johnson, the younger, named in William Scudder's Will of July 27, 1607 and proved November 4, 1607 was the same John Johnson who married Mary Heath in Ware, Hertfordshire, England. [11] There are no marriage records in Darenth or Wilmington, Kent County, England for a Margaret (Margery) Scudder and a John Johnson nor a marriage record for a Margaret (Margery) Stacey and a John Johnson.

The first Scudders who arrived in the Massachusetts Bay Colony arrived in 1634. The first was Thomas Scudder of Darenth who settled in Salem, Massachusetts, William Scudder of Darenth who settled also in Salem, Massachusetts, and John Scudder who arrived on the ship '*James*' from London in 1635 and settled in Charleston, Massachusetts. [12]

It is the belief of the author that John Johnson married PRIOR to immigrating to America in 1630. However, examination of the Boyd Marriage Index in England and those records of parishes where John Johnson lived and was likely to have lived did not reveal any marriage of a John Johnson to any Margery.

Virtually every genealogical book regarding John Johnson's second marriage is wrong.

Likewise, ALL second marriage information (Margery Scudder) for John Johnson on the webpages on the Internet are in error. Furthermore, records submitted by members of the Church of Jesus Christ, Latter Day Saints in the Family History Center's IGI and Ancestral File are wrong as they pertain to the 2nd marriage of Captain John Johnson of Roxbury, Massachusetts. There are no records that support the notion that Margery Scudder was married to John Johnson. It is believed that many later genealogists have merely copied previously erroneous genealogical information and have passed such information on.

CHAPTER SEVEN

THE CHURCHES OF JOHN JOHNSON

John Johnson and his first wife, Mary Heath Johnson, were married in Ware, Hertfordshire, England, in the St. Mary the Virgin Church on September 21, 1613. It was an Anglican Church, a Church of England. [1] The St. Mary the Virgin Church as it now appears has been in continuous use since 1400 A.D. but the original Church dated back to at least 1078 A.D.

St. Mary the Virgin Church, Ware, England

The dimensions of the present church were given in The Builder, December 1847, as follows:

Length of Nave	81 feet
Width	21 feet
Whole width of church inside	53 feet, 6 inches
Chancel	40 feet x 23 feet
Tower height	78 feet
Spire	30 feet

Seating capacity for St. Mary the Virgin Church was approximately 500. [2]

Children of John and Mary Heath Johnson who were baptized in the St. Mary the Virgin Church were: [3]

Mary Johnson	July 31, 1614
Sarah Johnson	November 12, 1624

Joseph Johnson	March 6, 1626/7*
Hannah Johnson	March 23, 1627/8*

*dates reflect change from Julian calendar to the Gregorian calendar

By the year 1558, the English Reformation caused St. Mary the Virgin Church to lose its internal beauty.[4]   Further removal of "things Catholic" occurred during the reign of King Henry VIII, who in 1529, began the process through parliamentary legislation to change the Roman Catholic Churches to Churches of England with he himself as head of the English Church instead of the Roman Catholic Pope Clement VII.

It is not recorded in any St. Mary the Virgin Church records of any responsibility or activity John Johnson or Mary Heath Johnson performed on behalf of the Church. For example, no bequeaths were made to the Church by any Johnson or Heath. Furthermore, there were no burials inside the Church of any Johnson or Heath. Mary Heath Johnson, of course, was buried in the Churchyard at St. Mary the Virgin as well as John and Mary Heath Johnson's children: John (July 6, 1627), Susan (August 16, 1629), and Joseph (March 30, 1627).

It should be pointed out that even though some of the children of John and Mary Heath Johnson were baptized at St. John the Baptist Church in Great Amwell, Hertfordshire, England, those children who died were buried at St. Mary the Virgin in Ware.

Because the author knows that John Johnson was a yeoman or farmer, it had been hoped that land records could be located to show ownership or leasing of lands in Ware and Great Amwell, which might have provided the clues to why children of John and Mary Heath Johnson were baptized in two different Churches. Records, unfortunately, were not located. However, it was a common practice for farmers to have lands in various places with residential dwellings on each parcel of land.

The St. John the Baptist Church in Great Amwell, Hertfordshire, England was the setting for baptisms for other children of John and Mary Heath Johnson.

Namely, the children baptized there were:

> Isaac Johnson, February 11, 1615
>
> John Johnson, April 5, 1618
>
> Elizabeth Johnson, August 22, 1619
>
> Humphrey Johnson, November 5, 1620
>
> Joseph Johnson, April 20, 1622
>
> Susan Johnson, July 16, 1623 [5]

St. John the Baptist Church is located in the tiny village of Great Amwell. The Church was built in the 700's A.D. with the additions of a rounded Apse in 1100 A.D. following the Norman invasion, and a tower in 1500 A.D. The Church, which is still in use, is surrounded by gravestones on all sides among many yew and cypress trees that were common in burial grounds.

St. John the Baptist Church in Great Amwell, England

The Church is located directly adjacent to the New River Lee (Lea) channel built between 1609-1613, which, as an artificial channel, carried fresh water to North London.

The Parish Register and Tithing Book of Thomas Hassall of Amwell reveals that its vicar, Thomas Hassall, served St. John the Baptist Church in Great Amwell from 1600 to 1657. He was a committed member of the National Church, the Church of England. [6] This statement will have further implications later as the religion of John Johnson is explored.

The Hassall book is a tremendous collection of every day happenings in Great Amwell. Essentially, Reverend Thomas

Hassall recorded all baptisms, marriages and deaths for a considerably long period of time. Strangely missing from Hassall's account, however, is the effect of Puritanism and the loss of membership because of emigration of some members to America beginning in 1630.

The question about why John Johnson, the Puritan, continued to have his children baptized in the Church of England has been partially explained by Professor Roger Thompson of East Anglia University in England. He has theorized that even strong Puritans adhered to *some* elements of the Anglican Church such as the rites of Communion, baptism, burial, and marriage. The Puritans, however, discarded such things as Christmas, Easter, All Saints' Days, and some fasting days. It is Thompson's belief that Puritans in the early Seventeenth Century *were provided for* by the Anglican Church *but in some less degree and formality* than other loyal members of the Church of England.

The reason that this has been a question is because John Johnson had long association with other Non-Conformist Puritans from Essex and Hertfordshire Counties in England as well as the fact that he was a founder of the First Church of Roxbury, Massachusetts. Further, John Johnson was instrumental in calling Reverend John Eliot, a fellow Non-Conformist, to be the pastor of the Roxbury Church. Yet, literally up to the time of emigration, John Johnson benefited from the Church of England in various ways such as baptisms and burials.

A Non-Conforming Puritan, is one who was neither a Non-Separatist nor a Separatist. Non-Separatists were individuals who wanted changes in the Church of England but did not want to separate from it. A Separatist wanted to separate from the Church of England to form a different type of Protestant Church such as Congregational. But a Non-Conformist Puritan not only wanted to separate from the Church of England, but also wanted to have a Church that was more strict, conservative, and pure than any other Protestant Church.

Early residents of Roxbury (1630-1631) were invited to worship with members of the First Church of Dorchester since Roxbury Puritans had not yet built a Church, which was originally called a *Meeting House*. While the Roxbury residents were attending Church in Dorchester, George Alcock was chosen their deacon. John Johnson attended the Dorchester Church, built in 1630, until the First Church of Roxbury, Massachusetts was built between 1631 and 1632.

Dorchester, Massachusetts was approximately one mile from the town of Roxbury. Both towns in the 1860's were incorporated into Boston. Roxbury people attended the Dorchester Church when weather permitted by using paths through the forests.

Since the beginning of the First Church of Roxbury, the Church has been located on the same spot without any breaks in its records, or any pause in its worship. The first Church edifice was built during 1631-32 as a tablet under the clock in the gallery of the present Meeting House reads, "This Church was gathered in 1632." [7,8] The first pastor was the Reverend Thomas Welde. [Weld] By 1632 another large group of Non-Conformist emigrants arrived from areas near Nazing, county of Essex, England. Many of these emigrants settled in Roxbury and were friends of Reverend John Eliot who had been called to provide pastoral care and teaching.

The first Meeting House was large enough to seat 120 persons. If it was like any of the first six New England Meeting Houses, it was an oblong building with a thatched roof. Men and women sat apart on their respective sides of the Meeting House.

Two services were held on Sundays, in the morning and afternoon, with a short interval between. It was a common service practice to give individual public thanksgiving to God but it was also a practice to provide discipline, public humiliation, repentance, and even ex-communication for errant members for civil or religious offenses.

The Meeting House was the setting where all matters relating to the Church or Community were transacted. Religious and Civil affairs were closely interlocked for the first seventy years of the Colonial Period (1630-1700).

During the past three-hundred and seventy years, five Churches or Meeting Houses have been located on the site of the first Church: [9]

First Church erected in 1631	(razed)
Second Church erected in 1674	(razed)
Third Church erected in 1740	(burned)
Fourth Church erected in 1744	(razed)
Fifth Church erected in 1804	(existing)

Principle founders of the First Church of Roxbury, Massachusetts were: [10]

William Pinchon	Isaac Morrill
George Alcock	John Ruggles
Thomas Lamb	Ralph Hemingway
John Johnson	Robert Williams
Griffeth Crafts	John Gore
William Dennison	John May
William Curtis	Edward Denison

[Note: In the Annals of New England, Part II, by Thomas Prince, cited below, Prince says that seventeen males were admitted first to the Roxbury Church.]

Thomas Prince, author of the Annals of New England (1755) pointed out that the first seventeen members of the Roxbury Church were *males* but by July 1632, seventeen females were admitted for membership followed by thirteen males. [11]   After 1632, there appears to be mixed gender lists. Whether the admittance of males only in the beginning of the Roxbury Church was a reflection upon the Puritan beliefs is not made clear. By 1643, some females were admitted to the Roxbury Church followed in later years by their husbands.

Unfortunately, because John Johnson's house burned down in 1645, much of the early history and records of the Church were destroyed. John Johnson was the Clerk of Roxbury and as such was the keeper of all civil and religious records.

Thwing, in his book, states, "that the creed has changed but the Church survives." [12] The 1908 quote seem to reflect an acknowledgment of the fall of the Puritan Society.

Since there was little distinction between religious and civil affairs, John Johnson and others on behalf of the Church, developed a covenant to establish in 1645 a "free grammar school" in Roxbury. It was known as *The Free Schoole in Roxburie"* and its purpose was to teach young people how to read so they could understand the Bible. All residents of Roxbury were taxed for the school expenses as well as expenses for the Church. Even the salary of the pastors of the Church was supported by taxation of ALL residents in Roxbury. This was possible, of course, because any persons who were non-believers or who were more liberal in religious thought and practice already had been banished from the Massachusetts Bay Colony.

CHAPTER EIGHT

THE ANCESTRY OF JOHN JOHNSON

John Johnson did not leave a shred of evidence where he was born in England. Charles E. Banks, who documented emigrants who came in the 1630 Winthrop Fleet, was not accurate in many birthplaces of these emigrants because he relied upon places of last residence before departure to New England. And in some cases, he used the point of departure of the ships in the Winthrop Fleet. Historians, such as Pope, Holmes, Drake, Coldham and others, have based the birthplace of the early Colonists on similar misinformation.

Likewise, every genealogist who has written the family genealogy of John Johnson has made the same errors about his ancestry or has made questionable speculation about it.

Erroneous information abounds in at least a dozen professional and amateur genealogies as well as genealogies on the Internet. In addition, there are errors are in Ancestral Files and Individual Genealogical Index files (IGI) that have been submitted by members of the Church of Jesus Christ of Latter Day Saints (LDS) who made conclusions much of which was based on previously written genealogies that they assumed were correct.

The author recognizes that erroneous information will be perpetuated regardless of this particular book. However, an examination of each "suspect" genealogy is studied below. Readers are asked to keep these speculative genealogies in mind as they develop their own theories about the genealogy of Captain John Johnson of Roxbury, Massachusetts.

Theory #1

Isaac Johnson and Lady Arbella Fiennes of Lincolnshire were the parents of John Johnson.

Isaac Johnson was born in 1601 in Semprington, Lincolnshire, England. He married Lady Arbella Fiennes, daughter of the Earl of Lincolnshire. Isaac Johnson's father and mother were Abraham Johnson and Anne Meadows Johnson. Isaac Johnson and Arbella Fiennes only had one descendant, Mary Johnson, who died as a child. [1, 2]

John Johnson was married to Mary Heath in Ware, Hertfordshire, England on September 21, 1613. His birth year is estimated to be c. 1585-1593.

If Isaac Johnson was born in 1601, and John Johnson was married in 1613, there is NO WAY that Isaac Johnson and Arbella Fiennes were the parents of John Johnson. John Johnson could not have been twelve years old or younger at the time of his marriage to Mary Heath.

Furthermore, both Isaac Johnson and Arbella died soon after their arrival to New England in 1630. The Will of Isaac Johnson in New England clearly establishes that he and Lady Arbella Fiennes had no living issue.

Theory #2

John Johnson's father was John Johnson of Wilmington, Kent, England because (a) his wife was Margery Scudder who was named in the will of John Lowers of Darenth, Kent, England, and, (b) in which it names a John Johnson, the elder and a John Johnson, the younger (Presumably, "our" Captain John Johnson) in the 1650 will.

First of all, John Johnson did NOT marry Margery Scudder. Margery Scudder, who was actually "Margaret Scudder" was married to Thomas Stacey who outlived her.

Part of this speculation has come from the Charles Banks' <u>Winthrop Fleet of 1630</u> book in which he believed that John Johnson emigrated from Wilmington, Kent, England. In their hurry to nail down John Johnson's ancestry, genealogists tried to put two and two together and came up with a somewhat believable assumption.

The glee of Emily C. Landon in her book, <u>Pepper Family</u> (Elizabeth Johnson, daughter of Captain John Johnson, married Robert Pepper) literally rings out when she stated:

> "Since our Thomas Scudder of Salem (1648) had children named John, Thomas, Henry, William and Elizabeth, I cannot but think I have found traces of his [John Johnson's] family in the above [meaning the William Scudder will] will." [3]

The will states: "To John Johnson the younger twenty shillings, both of the parish of Wilmington......."

Furthermore, a study of the county of Kent birth and death records K-91433; #1553186 dated August 30, 1988 (LDS Family History Center) and #1836276 dated June 1, 1992, roll 289, England 54000, Kent, did not reveal any John Johnson being born to a John

Johnson. Further, there is no record of a John Johnson birth in Herne or Herne Hill parish, Kent, England.

Captain Edward Johnson of Woburn, Massachusetts WAS from Herne Hill, Kent, England. There is no evidence, however, that Edward Johnson and John Johnson were related. Moreover, when Captain Edward Johnson gave an account of the importance of Captain John Johnson on learning of his death, Captain Edward Johnson did not indicate *any kinship* such as brother or cousin.

It is concluded that Captain John Johnson of Roxbury, Massachusetts was not born in either Wilmington, England or Herne Hill, England [sometimes referred to as Herne Bay] based upon actual readings of the parish records in both parishes.

Theory #3

John Johnson's father and mother were Francis Johnson and Elizabeth Thorogood Johnson.

The dates are all wrong for these people to be the parents of Captain John Johnson. The mother of Elizabeth Thorogood was Cecily (Cecilia) Baynam. Baynam would have been only four years old when her supposed grandson, John Johnson, was born c. 1590.

Theory #4

John Johnson was the son of John Johnson, born about 1570, and Hannah Throckmorton.

[John Johnson, b. c. 1590, is sometimes listed in the IGI as <u>husband</u> of Hannah Throckmorton in addition to being cited also as a <u>son</u> of Hannah Throckmorton.]

The birth date of 1588, Langton, Lincolnshire, England submitted by a Mr. Richard Miner to the Ancestral Files, is not listed in any of the Lincolnshire parish records of births. In regard to the submitted material, a private letter dated April 5, 1999 to the author, Richard Miner of Springville, Utah indicated that he had inherited the research of his mother and that of the Aaron Johnson Family Organization. Believing that the information researched by his mother was correct, Mr. Miner submitted the information to the Ancestral Files of the Family History Center of the LDS Church.

Theory #5

John Johnson's father was John Johnson and grandparents were Geoffrey Johnson and Bridgett Harbottle.

Neither Geoffrey Johnson, son of Maurice Johnson, nor Bridgett Harbottle, wife of Geoffrey Johnson are listed in any of the Herne Hill, Kent, England parish records in the 1500s. Geoffrey Johnson, if related, would have been a grandfather, not a father, of our Captain John Johnson. He died September 1585 at age 60 in Leicester, England. Ms. Lynda Hotchkiss, genealogist for the county of Lincolnshire Council Genealogical Research Service, extensively researched this connection in November 1998. Ms. Hotchkiss clearly establishes that John Johnson and Isaac Johnson were NOT brothers as all sources clearly show "Abraham, father of Isaac Johnson, had no son John." [4] Maurice Johnson, father of

Robert Johnson and grandfather of Abraham Johnson, was married three times with the last marriage being in Rutland. According to Ms. Hotchkiss this suggests other children but she did not find any definite leads to a John Johnson who could have married in 1613 in Ware, Hertfordshire, England.

The Rutland visitation of 1618/19 lists several sons for Geoffrey Johnson including a John Johnson. However, no dates were given. This particular John Johnson was admitted to Grays Inn on November 16, 1586 from Staple Inn (law schools) and had graduated from St. John's in Michelmas, Cambridge University in 1589. It is believed that these dates would make this John Johnson too early for the birth of Captain John Johnson of Roxbury. However, Ms. Hotchkiss suggests that "IF there is a link between the two Johnsons (Isaac and John) who went to America, it may be through the patronage of various people, and family which is why she suggests that the possibility that John is the son [she may have meant grandson] of Geoffrey Johnson." [5]

Theory #6

Cited in the IGI is a John Johnson whose father and mother were John Johnson and Alice Prior of Ware, Hertfordshire, England. [A John Johnson was born 1636, Ware, Hertfordshire, England to John and Alice Prior.]

Captain John Johnson is already in America [1630] when this John Johnson was born in Ware, Hertfordshire, England. Thus, he is NOT our Captain John Johnson.

Theory #7

*The father of John Johnson of Roxbury,
Massachusetts was William Johnson of Watford,
Hertfordshire, England.*

There actually is a christening of a John Johnson on December 15,
1588, St. Mary's Parish, Watford, Hertfordshire, England. The
christening date is listed within LDS Film Batch number CO73O51.

There is no further evidence that this John Johnson of Watford,
Hertfordshire, England is our Captain John Johnson of Roxbury.
The distance between Watford and Ware, though not an
impossibility, was inconsistent with the movement and the marriage
patterns in the Seventeenth Century in England. Marriages were
usually within three or four parishes between spouses.

Since three years of research have not resulted in the identification
of the ancestry nor the birth date or place of John Johnson, the
following is a listing to serve as a resource aid for future
genealogists and historians.

While many records have virtually disappeared, or as one English
genealogist said, "the fate of some records were probably destroyed
by mold and rats in the various parishes," this listing may be helpful
to others should additional records be found.

1. Johnson marriages in the county of Middlesex (possible parents
    of John Johnson ONLY if John Johnson's hometown was more
    than four parishes away from Ware, Hertfordshire:

    Boyd Marriage Index, both series

1561	Johnson and Joan Marshall, St. Dunstan E.
1566	Johnson and Ethelred Backford, Dunstan W.
1566	Johnson and Luce Simms, Mary Adermanbury
1570	Johnson and Jane Davis, James Garlichithe

1570   Johnson and Agnes Cook, St. Dunstan E
1571   Johnson and Catherine Castleforth, And Undershot
1572   Johnson and Agnes Gladwine, Gilston Herts
1575   Johnson and Elizabeth Seabroke, Hemel Hempstead, Herts
1575   Johnson and Joan Stone, Faversham, Kent BT
1576   Johnson and Joan Freir, Eastington Gloustershire
1576   Johnson and Joan Boldren, Bp London
1577   Johnson and Catherine Goodieare, Clareboro Notts
1577   Johnson and Elizabeth Haw, Bedale Yorks
1579   Johnson and Elianor ____, Broadwinsor Dorset
1579   Johnson and Margaret Fandry, Kiddington Oxon
1580   Johnsonand Elizabeth Fry, Clifford Chambers Glos
1583   Johnson and Mathie Pexton, Mary at Hill
1583   Johnson and Fran Ellis, Canterbury
1583   Johnson and Em Raty, Salisbury
1586   Johnson and Ann Bennet, James Garlickhithe
1586   Johnson and Joan Perseval, Lymm Chesire
1588   Johnson and Elizabeth Hamlet, Ste Cleman
1588   Johnson and Ann Wite, Alvingham Lincolnshire
1590   Johnson John Johnson and Jane Smith, Kingston Surrey
1590   Johnson and Mary Bird, Mary at Hill
1591   Johnson and Mary Willes, Canterbury
1591   Johnson and Eln Farley, Paver
1591   Johnson and Joan Love, Wantage Berks
1592   Johnson and Mary Peter, Kath Tower
1592   Johnson and Catherine Tillett, Ramsey Hunts
1592   Johnson and Alice Goodwin, Ansty Lincolnshire
1592   Johnson and Jud Hall, James Garlickithe
1593   Johnson and Joan Smith, Thornbury Glos

2. Johnson marriages in county of Essex (possible parents of John Johnson ONLY if John Johnson's hometown was three or four parishes away from Ware, Hertfordshire):

    1563   Johnson and Joan Pain, Cleavering

    1566   Johnson and Abigail _____, Romford

    1567   Johnson and Joan Haires, W. Hanningfield

    1571   Johnson and Agnes Night, Lt. Baddow

    1573   Johnson and Marie Lewkner, Magdalen Laver

    1575   Johnson and Elizabeth Brown, Mashbury

    1578   Johnson and Elinor Roberteson, Harwich

    1580   Johnson and Sarah Spooner, Gt. Leighs

    1581   Johnson and Barbara Brook, Burnham

    1582   Johnson and Joan Awcoke, W. Tilbury

    1585   Johnson and Ann Clark, Theydon Mount

    1588   Johnson and Mary Edmondes, Leyton

    1590   Johnson and Alice Andrew, Colchester Mary Walls

    1592   Johnson and Joan Chignell, Thaxted

    1594   Johnson and Joan Cramphorn, Burnham

3. Johnson marriages, Lt. Waltham, county of Essex

No Johnson marriages, 1595-1625

4. Johnson marriages, Waltham Abbey, county of Essex

No Johnson marriages, 1595-1625
No Johnson Christenings, 1570-1605

5. Johnson marriages, Waltham Holy Cross, county of Essex (possible parents of John Johnson) Waltham Holy Cross is approximtely 12 miles north of London:

    1577 Nycolas Johnson and Agnes Homes

6. Waltham Holy Cross, county of Essex (Possible siblings of John Johnson)

    Thomas, son of Nycolas Johnson, christened Nov. 24, 1577

    John, son of Nycolas Johnson, christened May 17, 1574 (1579) [perhaps a good lead yet considered to be too early for the birth of our John Johnson]

7. county of Essex parishes bordering Hertfordshire:

    Waltham Holy Cross (Waltham Abbey), Nazeing, Epping, Roydon, Great Parndon, Netteswell, Latton

8. Inns of Court Lists

    Lincolns Inn, 1586-1660
        Mr. Johnson, Nov. 25, 1606
        [likely too early for our John Johnson]

        Abraham Johnson, 1594
        Frederic Johnson, 1598
        Matthias Johnson
        Robert Johnson
        Thomas Johnson, 1593
        William Johnson, 1605

Grays Inn, 1575-1630 Admissions

    1578 William Johnson
    1586 John Johnson
    1605 William Johnson
    1607 William Johnson
    1618 Richard Johnson
    1618 Alexander Johnson
    1621 Isaack Johnson
    1629 Morgan Johnson
    1634 John Johnson

Middle Temple, 1501-1781 Admissions:

    1557 William Johnson
    1557 Robert Johnson
    1564 Richard Johnson
    1577 Thomas Johnson
    1591 John Johnson
    1595 Isaac Johnson
    1611 Ambrose Johnson
    1614 William Johnson

Inner Temple, 1595-1635 Admissions

    1599 Robert Johnson
    1609 Edward Johnson
    1621 Thomas Johnson
    1622 Lancelot Johnson
    1626 John Johnson
    1642 George Johnson

Barnards Inn, 1620-1869, Admissions

1627, Richard Johnson
(no John Johnsons listed)

9. Lay Subsidies, Elizabeth era, E-179, Hertfordshire, 1575-1650

No Johnson found for Hertford Hundred (Amwell) or for Broughing Hundred (Ware)

10. Lay Subsidies, Vol. III, p. 130, Hertfordshire

Lay Tax Subsidies checked for periods James I, 1604/5 to Charles I, 1626/7.

11. Victoria County History of Hertfordshire (Johnsons)

Audrey Johnson

C. Johnson

Edward Johnson

Elizabeth Johnson

Frances Johnson

Grace Johnson

Henry Johnson

John Johnson, basketmaker, Wormley

John Johnson, Sawbridgeworth, a married priest and school master, 1554 (date would dictate that this John Johnson would have to be subject John Johnson's *grandfather*, not father)

J. Henry Johnson

Martin Johnson

Maurice Johnson, 1688-1755, eldest son of Maurice Johnson, barrister of Inner Temple (Lincolnshire Johnsons)

Robert Johnson

Thomas Johnson

William Johnson

W. Johnson

Dr. Johnson

R.E. Johnston

12. Allen Marriage Index of Hertfordshire from the earliest surviving records to 1837:

John Johnson and Isabel Dagnole, 1600 Aldenham

John Johnson and Mary Heath, 1613, Ware
(subject of this book)

John Johnson and Joice Dode, Abbey, 1610

John Johnson and Alice Dowse, M. Hadham, 1610

John Johnson and Hannah Therfield, 1619

John Johnson and Ann Lowen, Cheshunt, 1628

13. Manorial Documents, 16-17th Centuries, Manorial Documents at Hertford CRO, 1550-1650:

No reference to any John Johnson

14. Index to Little Amwell Court Rolls "Elizabeth to 1711":

No Johnsons until 1691

15. Broxborune Court Rolls, Volume 12, 1628/9

No Johnsons found

16. Elizabethan Life: Essex Gentry Wills Proved PCC

Elizabeth 249	1574 20/ from George Sayer of Colchester
Henry 271	1568 witness Halstead
Henry 297	1673 one cow pasturing Halstead
Henry 303	1572 parson of Mistley
Henry 188	1571 parson of Mistley
Joyce 28	1577 maiden of Dame Jane Newtes
Margaret 28	1577 Mistress Margaret Johnson of Bedlam left holland sheets by Dame Jane Newtes
Sam 274	1573 servant to alderman John Beaste of Colchester
William 282	1590 witness Walthamstow
Goodman 240	1584 of Chingford

17. Elizabethan Life: Morals and the Church Courts in the county of Essex

Joan Johnson 35	1574 Kelvedon
John Johnson 30	1591 Edward Benbrick of West Ham at request of John Johnson of Bow, his own aunt's wife's…..
Osias Johnson 37	1590s married by license from Commissary of Essex to Patience Dowdale of St. Leonard's Colchester aged 22; clothier of

74

Kelvedon

William Johnson rector of Chignal St. James instituted 1555

18. county of Essex Wills, Vol. 1; 1558-1565 (Archdeaconry of Essex, Archdeaconry of Colchester, Archdeaconry of Middlesex, Essex and Herts Division:

Agnes Johnson 239 1559 will of husband Thomas of Orsett

Agnes Johnson 562 1562 widow witness to will of Isabel Stevenson of Berkingside

Alice Johnson 513 1559 widow of Leonard Johnson of Thydon Garnon

Alice Johnson 896 1558/9 mother of Joan Catherine Johnson

19. Herts Genealogist and Antiquary - ed. William Brigg for Johnsons

Alice Johnson, dau. of William of Sawbridgeworth whose will January 15, 1570. He had two sons, Thomas and John Johnson

Anne, p. 236 and possibly p. 238

Elizabeth, p. 59

Elizabeth, p. 209 wife of John 1552, Watford, Herts

Etheldreda, p. 311, wife of Robert Johnson

Henry, p. 218

Henry, p. 238, proved Ware but of Braughing. Will, 1569

John Johnson, p. 39

John Johnson, p. 161, manors of Kingswoodbury, etc.

John Johnson of Stortford, p. 209

John Johnson of Wormley, 1545, p. 270

John Johnson, p. 271, Cheshunt Streate 1545, Lay Subsidy, John Johnson an alyen

John, p. 349, Ashwell 1545

Margery, p. 51 and p. 277

Marie p. 238

Nicholas p. 133 witness at Stanstead Abbots 1565 and 1567

Richard, p. 226, 1545

Robert, p. 20 and p. 278

Theordore, p. 196 deeds before us Th Johnson, 1719

Thomas, p. 108, 1558, St. Albans

Thomas, p. 110, 1562, St. Albans

Thomas, p. 201, deeds, 1548 Sandridge

Thomas, p. 228, 1545 Aldenham

Thomas, p. 246, Sawbridgeworth

William, p. 57

William, p. 111, St. Albans Holywell

William, p. 273, Waltham, 1545

William, p. 230, Hitchin, 1545

William, p. 333, Will, of Sawbridgeworth proved at Stortford Feb. 14, 1570/1 daughter Alice, sons, Thomas and John

William, p. 349, Ashwell, 1545

William, p. 350, Royston

20. Herts Genealogist and Antiquary - ed. William Brigg (Volume 2) for Johnsons

Ann, p. 9
Ann, p. 53
Alice, p. 63
Elizabeth, p. 210
Grace, p. 77, 1570
Henry, p. 63

Henry, p. 81, Datchworth and manor, 1571

Henry, Sawbridgeworth, 1579

Henry, p. 344, Sawbridgeworth, 1585

James, p. 135, Hoddesdon 1573

James, p. 175, Hoddesdon, 1574

John, p. 237

John, p. 353, 1545, Hexton

John, bp London Consistory Court. August 7, 1592. John of Wormley basketmaker, sons William and John. Grandchildren Joan, John and Richard; Ann Johnson, and Alice Johnson

Mary, p. 9

Nicholas, p. 132. St. Albans, 1572

Nicholas, p. 274, Stanstead, 1574

Richard, p. 9

Richard, p. 166

Richard, p. 346, St. Alban Middleward

Richard, p. 353, 1545 Codicote Richard Johnson

Robert, p. 66, writer, St. Albans, 1601

Roger, p. 349, 1545, Rickmansworth Towne

Thomas, p. 37; lands at Sawbridgeworth

Thomas, p. 237 Archdy St. Albans

William, p. 21

William, p. 53

William, p. 164

William, p. 237

William, p. 349, Richmansworth Towne, 1545

22. Herts Genealogist and Antiquary - ed. William Brigg (Volume 3 for Johnsons)

>Brian, p. 153, Rickmanworth, son Thomas, 1570
>
>Brian, p. 153 Rickmansworth
>
>Catherine, p. 133, St. Peters
>
>Elizabeth, p. 133, St. Peters
>
>John, p. 143, lands, Totteridge with wife Susan, 1592
>
>Richard, Gentleman, p. 3, Mich, 1586, manor of Garnons and lands, Great Munden
>
>Susan, p. 143, wife of John, 1592
>
>Thomas, p. 52, 1566, gentleman in Harpenden
>
>Thomas, p. 153, see Brian above
>
>William, p. 69, Tring Magna manor Court rolls, 1621
>
>William, p. 133, St. Peters

24. Miscellanea (Was Roxbury, MA named after an English town or village?)

a) county of Essex: Rochford - the name of a Hundred and of a parish. The form Rokesford occurs: it would be similar to Roxford.

b) county of Hertfordshire: Roxford - a district in Hertingfordbury, which is a parish adjoining Hertford, county of Hertfordshire.

c) Widford - There is a Widford near Ware, in Hertfordshire, and another in Essex in Chelmsford Hundred with some evidence for Johnsons in both places.

d) Little Baddow - county of Essex - near Chelmsford. A connection between Reverend John Eliot who lived in Little Baddow and John Johnson is not impossible. [In 1631, citizens, including John Johnson of Roxbury, MA, called Rev. John Eliot to be the minister of the First Church of Roxbury.]

(e) Roxwell - county of Essex - about 18 miles east of Ware (Hertfordshire) toward Chelmsford (county center of Essex)

25. Miscellanea: Paul Franklin Johnson wrote in his <u>Genealogy of Captain John Johnson of Roxbury, MA</u> that John Johnson was from "12 miles from London on the river Lee." (What towns or villages might be 12 miles from London on the river Lee in 1630?)

> On the Hertfordshire-Essex county borders: Cheshunt and Waltham with Wormley a mile or two further. Ware, where John Johnson married Mary Heath, is 21 miles from London as well as is Great Amwell. While many nonconformists did not always have their children christened in the parish church, it appears that John Johnson and Mary Heath Johnson's children were baptized in the churches of the parishes where they lived.

26. <u>Additional East Hertfordshire towns where Johnsons married, 1580-1630 (possible parents of John Johnson **ONLY** if John Johnson's hometown was within four parishes of Ware)</u>:

Great Amwell:
> 1580 Thomas Johnson and Alice Briggs (Brigges)
> 1591 John Archer and Alice Johnson

Bayford:
> No Johnson marriages, 1580 - 1630

Bengeo:
> 1610 Robert Johnson and Anna Woodde

Bramfield:
No Johnson marriages, 1580-1630

Broxbourne/Hoddesdon: no registers before 1688

Hertingfordbury:
No marriage registers before 1679
Birth records, 1604-1624
No Johnsons listed

Hertford All Saints:
1587 Thomas Johnson and Elizabeth Parkin
1611 Martin Johnson and Elizabeth Pen (Penn)
1616 Robert Simmons and Anne Johnson
1629 John Rutt and Joan Johnson

Hertford St. Andrews:
1595   Rafe Johnson and Ann Croutch
1596   Rafe Johnson and Clare Clifford
1609 Thomas Master and Agnes Johnson
1619 Chpr Clefford and Jane Johnson

Hunsdon: from Gibbs transcripts
1628 Reinold Eliot and Joane Johnson

Sacombe:
No marriage registers before 18th Century

Stanstead Abbots:
No marriage registers before 1679

Stanstead St. Margarets:
No marriage registers before 1697

Thundrige from Kemmis transcripts at Hertford Museum:
No Johnson marriages 1580-1630

Ware:

    1599 John Johnson and Frances Skyngle

    1602 Hy Johnson and Sat Archer

    1608 Thomas Johnson and Sarah Shawe

    1610 Thomas Johnson and Susan Connies

    1613 John Johnson and Mary Heath [subject of this book]

    1613 Laur Johnson and Dorcas Nele

    1621 George Wood and Elizabeth Johnson

    1625 George Johnson and Ann Downes

    1625 Robert Johnson and Joan Watts

    1629 Richard Barker and Rose Johnson

Widford:

    1614 Thomas Johnson and Katherine Thirkell both of Ware

    1622 Richard Taylor (als Charles) and Agnes Johnson

27. Some conclusions based upon prior research, and the findings in the year 2000:

If John Johnson followed the pattern of marriages in the Seventeenth Century, he would not have lived more than three or four parishes away from Mary Heath, Ware.

Possible parents, then, of John Johnson could be:

a) Thomas Johnson and Elizabeth Parkin, married 1587, Hertford All Saints

b) Thomas Johnson and Alice Briggs, married 1580, Great Amwell

c) William Johnson and _____, married prior to 1588, Watford St. Marys

d) Thomas Johnson and Joane _____ [Lived in Great Amwell prior to 1619. Joan Johnson of Hodesdon End died January 10, 1619]

81

Possible birth towns of John Johnson based upon the possibility than John Johnson married Mary Heath from **three or four parishes away from Ware, Hertfordshire** (Herts):

> Watford - Herts

a) Great Amwell - Herts
b) Ware - Herts
c) Sawbridgeworth - Herts
d) Hertford - Herts
e) Waltham - Essex
f) Cheshunt - Essex
g) Wormley - Essex
h) Burnham - Essex
i) Nazeing/Waltham Half Hundred - Essex
j) Waltham Holy Cross/Waltham Abbey- Essex
k) Hertingfordbury - Essex
n) Hodesdon - Herts

Because John Johnson appeared to have an education and work experience perhaps reflecting a family of money and travel, some have counseled the author that John Johnson could have traveled further than three or four parishes from Ware in order to marry Mary Heath and to work. The most frequent example given is that of John Winthrop (at an early age) who traveled a great distance to marry his first wife.

[Note: See also item # 42 in this Chapter.]

28. <u>Ware manor of Waters als Mardock (Court Rolls of Charles I document 10826)</u>

No Johnson was found in these court rolls

29. Monumental Inscriptions in Ware Churchyard and Church (St. Mary the Virgin); copied c. 1900 by Archibald Bannister

   No Johnson was found

30. Ware Vestry Minutes (to see if John Johnson was listed in any Church records)

   These records do not exists prior to 1704.

31. Ware Burials from mss t/s at Society of Genealogists in London

Sep 25, 1559	Thomas Jonson
Jan 17, 1559/60	Margaret Johnson
Apr 13, 1562	William Johnson
Dec 25, 1574	William Johnson
Nov 19, 1577	John Johnson
Jun 21, 1578	Agnes Johnson
Sep 16, 1587	Helen Johnson
May 11, 1590	Thomas Johnson
Sep 08, 1607	Catherine Johnson
Dec 02, 1608	Nicolas Johnson
Mar 13, 1611	Joane Johnson
Aug 23, 1611/12	John Johnson
Aug 25, 1613	Sarah Johnson
Nov 19, 1613	Thomas Johnson
Dec 25, 1613	Elizabeth Johnson
Aug 29, 1615	Susan Johnson
Jan 20, 1617/18	Clare Johnson
Mar 02, 1617/18	Ralph Johnson
Jun 05, 1619	Thomas Johnson

Aug 14, 1620	Agnes Johnson
Feb 02, 16222/3	Mary Johnson
May 02, 1622/3	Mary Johnson
Mar 30, 1627	Joseph Johnson
Jul 06, 1627	John Johnson
May 15, 1629	Mary Health Johnson
Aug 16, 1629	Susan Johnson

32. Ware Baptisms, 1558 from mss at Society of Genealogists, London

Jan 13, 1559/60	Margaret Johnson
Aug 24, 1561	John Johnson
Mar 24, 1565	Ellyn Johnson
Feb 06, 1568/9	Andrew Johnson
Feb 10, 1571/2	Robert Johnson
Mar 13, 1585/6	Margaret Johnson

33. Male Johnson Marriages at Ware, 1558 - December 1632 (from mss t/s at Society of Genealogists, London

May 28, 1599	John Johnson and Frances Skyngle
May 13, 1602	Henry Johnson and Sarah Archer
Jun 05, 1608	Thomas Johnson and Sarah Shawe
Jun 03, 1610	Thomas Johnson and Susan Connies
Sep 21, 1613	John Johnson and Mary Heath (subject of this book)
Feb 16, 1613/4	Laurence Johnson and Dorcas Nele
Oct 26, 1625	George Johnson and Ann Downes
Nov 07, 1625	Robert Johnson and Joan Watts

34. Waltham Holy Cross/Waltham Abbey, Essex (Parish records t/s with index at Society of Genealogists, London):

p. 4   Bur Thomas Johnsonne the sonne of Thomas Johnson the 10 Dec 1563

p. 6   Chr William Johnsonne son of Wm Johnsone 21 Maye 1564

p. 9   Bap Henry Johnsonne the son of Henrye Johnsonne 19/29 Oct 1654

p. 21   Chr John Johnsonne the sonne of William Johnsonne 22 Dec 1566

p. 31   Bur Rebeckea Johnsonne the Daughter of Henry Johnson 21 Jul 1568

p. 40   Bur Elyzabeth Johnson the daughter of Henre Johnston 20 Dec 1569

p. 54   Chr George Johnson the sonne of Henry Johnson 20 Jan 1572

p. 74   Bur Elen Johnson the wyfe of Henry Johnson May 1575

p. 79   Chr Edward Johnson the son of Edward Johnson the XI Mar 1576

p. 80   Mar Henry Johnson and Catherine Taller, widow, 10 May 1576

p. 87   Mar Nycolas Johnson and Anges Homes 23 Aug 1577

p. 88   Chr Thomas Johnson the sonne of nycolas Johnson 24 Oct 1577

p. 94   Bur Rebecca, daughter of Henry Johnson, 1578

p. 94   Bur Denes Johnson the wyfe of henry Johnson, 19 Sep 1578

p. 95   John Johnson the sonne of Nycolas Johnson, 17 Maye 1579 (event not listed)

p. 109 Chr Robert Johnson s of Richarde Johnson 22 Nov

1581

p. 111   Bap William Johnson the son of Rycharde Johnson 27 May 1582

p. 132   Mar John Vincent? Everet? And Joan Johnson 25 Nov 1585

p. 141   Bap Marion Johnson d Henrye Johnson, 16 Jul 1587

p. 154   Bur Alce Johnson wyfe of Robert Johnson 9 Sep 1589

p. 159   Bur Joan Johnson 20 Aug 1590

p. 172   Bur Robert Johnson 6 Nov 1592

p. 184   Bur Katherine Johnson, wwffe of John Nov 1595

p. 186   Bur Henry Johnson, butcher 15 Aug 1596

p. 190   Bur Anges Johnson, widow of Edward, 12 Jun 1597

p. 211   Mar John Johnson and Brigeat Shalforne 2 Nov 1600

35. Waltham Holy Cross (Waltham Abbey), Essex Probate Administration Commissary Court of London (possible parent (s) of John Johnson)

> Commissary Court of London (London Division) Calendar of wills, probate and administrations Acts 1603 - 1629 Microfilm 766 at Society of Genealogists, London, microfilm 761 registered wills 1660 + Microfilm 763 Dean and Chapter of St Pauls; microfilm 765 London Commissary Court, London Division wills and administration 1374- 1603; microfilm 766 reg 20; microfilm 767 London Commissary Court 1545+; microfilm 768 London Commissary Court wills and administration 1584-1638 index, Act Books 1639-1665, 1662-1689 index:

Bennet Johnson 22 Feb 1606 Reg 20 f.271

Daniel Johnson vintner London 20 Oct 1607 f. 325

John Johnson yeoman, Waltham Cross (Walthamstow) 1 Jul 1606 f. 108

Robert Johnson Merchant Taylor St. Bride 3 Jan 1607 f. 290

Robert Johnson 31 October 1606 f. 221

Thomas Johnson chip carpenter Whitechapel 11 Jun 1606 f. 177

William Johnson innholder London 22 Jun 1604 f. 56

Daniel Johnson St. Martin Vintry 1 Oct 1606 AB 16 f.2

Edward Johnson Stepney 10 Mar 1605 AB 16 f.22

Ellena Johnson als Evans St Stephen Coleman 26 Oct 1604 AB 15 f. 327

Lucas Johnson Stepney 9 May 1606 AB 16 f.25

Luca Johnson St. Mich Wood St 24 Apr 1607 AB 16 f. 47

Oliver Johnson alias Burrall Stepney 31 Mar 1604 AB 15 f. 312

Richard Johnson St. Bride 25 Nov 1607 AB 16 f. 57

Robert Johnson Stepney 15 Jul 1606 AB 16 f. 30

Henry Johnson St. Catherine Cree 23 Oct 1609 AB 16 f. 97

Henry Johnson Edmonton 19 Dec 1610 AB f. 22

James Johnson Whitechapel 28 Feb 1610 AB 16 f. 126

John Johnson St. Sepulchre 10 May 1608 AB 16 f. 83

John Johnson Whitechapel 3 May 1609 AB 16 f. 86

John Johnson de Witte Whitechapel 2 Nov 1610 AB 16 f. 120

John Johnson St. Stephen Coleman St 4 Jun 1611 AB 16 f. 131

Phillis Johnson Whitechapel 8 Mar 1607 AB 16 f. 63

William Johnson St Sepulchre de bon non 12 Dec 1609 AB

16 f. 101

Wills 1607 - 1611 reg. 21

Henry Johnson Merchant Taylor London 14 Nov 1609 reg 21 f. 193

Joanna Johnson widow All Hallows Staining 7 Jul 1610 f. 272

Robert Johnston St. Andrew Undershaft 30 Oct 1611 f. 363

Wills 1612 - 1621

Allin Johnson Edmonton 15 Oct 1617 23 f. 98

Edward Johnson Cit. Carpenter St. Sepulchre 17 May 1621 23 f. 503

Gilbert Johnson ship Charles Wapping 15 Oct 1621 28 f. 98

Isabel Johnson widow St. Brides 22 Jul 1613 22 f. 81

Jane Johnson widow Enfield 2 Aug 1619 23 f. 261

John Johnson husb St. Spulchre w't Newgate 5 Apr 1619 23 f. 261

John Johnson gentleman Layton Essex 26 Sep 1620 23 f. 531/532

Martin Johnson Stepney ship Charles 28 Sep 1618 23 f. 210

Peter Johnson Stepney ship Charles 28 Sep 1618 23 f. 210

William Johnson St. James Garlichithe 19 Jul 11616 22 f. 575

William Johnson yeoman Hamstead 6 Nov 1618 23 f.220

William Johnson Stepney 18 Oct 1621 24 f.35

Commissary Court of London (London Division) admons 1612-1621

Ann Johnson St. Andrew Hubbard 13 Jun 1620 AB 17 p. 46

Coletta Johnson St. martin Vintry 16 Mar 1613/14 AB 116 p. 192 ?

Cornelius Johnson St. Cathrerine Cree 16 Sep 1620 AB 16 p;. 262

Elizabeth Johnson St. Bride 1616 AB 16 p. 262

Elizabeth Johnson widow St. Stephen Coleman 1612 AB 16 p. 151

Garret Johnson St. Benet Fink 1612 AB 16 p. 159

Jaspar Johnson St. Lawrence Old Jewry 1616 AB 16 p. 260

John Johnson Whitechapel 1611/12 AB 16 142

John Johnson Stephney 1620 AB 17 p. 40

Lawrence Johnson Stephney 1621 AB 17 p. 72

Magnus Johnson Stepney 1620 AB 17 p. 37

Moses Johnson Stepney 1617 AB 16 p. 274

Robert Johnson St. Dunstan in W 1620 AB 17 p. 51

Roger Johnson St. Alban Wood St. 1613/14 AB 16 p. 191

Thomas Johnson Edmonton 1617/18 AB 16 p. 295

William Johnson Stepney 1614 AB 16 p. 206

William Johnson Christchurch London 1613/14 AB 16 p. 190

Wills, 1622-1625

Edward Johnson husb Greenford Magna Middx 24 Jan 1624 reg 24 f. 284

Elizabeth Johnson widow St. Mary Whitechapel 22 Jul 1623 24 f. 254

John Johnson St. Sepulchre 1625 24 f. 534

Michael Johnson mariner Limehouse 1625 24 f. 639

Thomas Johnson sailor on Claw died beyond seas 12625 24 f 326

William Johnson sailor Wapping 1624 24 f. 312

William Johnson St. Mary Whitechapel 1625 24 f. 504

Administrations

Isaac Johnson St. Catherine Cree 1622 17.97

James Johnson Edmonton 1624 17.167

James Johnson Whitechapel 1624 17.174

John Johnson St. Sepulchre 1623/4 17.160

John Johnson Stepney 1622.3 17.127

John Johnson St. Sepulchre 1625 17.193

John Johnson Stepney 1623 17.139

John Johnson St. Catherine Cree 1625 17.209

John Johnson Hackney 1625 17.227

Juniper Johnson Stepney 1625 17.227

Lawrence Johnson Ealing 1625 17.237

Thomas Johnson St. Sepulchre 1625 17.239

Ottawell Johnson Stepney 1622   17.101

Administrations 1626 - 1629

Barnard Johnson cordwainer St. Olave Southwark d. beyond seas Nov. 2, 1629

Samuel Johnson St. Giles Fields Aug 29, 1624

Thomas Johnson Cit and clothworker St. And Undershaft 1627 Mar 29, 1627

Thomas Johnson Cit and Fishmonger St. Nich Olave Apr 23, 1627

Anne Johnson, widow St. Martin Orgars

Benedicta Johnson St. Sepulchre Octr 28, 1626

Edward Johnson Stepney Middx Aug 15, 1629

Elizabeth Johnson Waltham Cross Essex (widow) Nov 21,

1627 reg 18.28

John Johnson All Hallows Barking Dec 18, 1629

Stephen Johnson St. martin Vintry Sep 13, 1626

36. Property Ownership, Hertfordshire; Ware/Amwell End deeds and estate papers dated before 1630.

10617 re Gaskynne land in Ware and Amwell. An Inquisition was held on 3 June 1628 at which Thomas Johnson of Amwell magna [meaning Great Amwell] was amongst those who "saye upon their oathes that Thomas Gaskyne (a tanner of Amwell) by his last will did gyve unto the poore people of Ware Amwell and Layston the yearly some of six shillings..."

37. Hertfordshire Militia Muster Books, 1580 - 1605 (listing of only Johnsons here)

1583

Barnarde Johnson Little Hadham

John Johnson trayned Hadham Magna

John Johnsonn carpenter

Artificers with their sonnes and servauntes

John Johnson carpenter trayned

1587

John Johnson furnished with the Towne Almayne Rivetes with Bills of Hadham Magna

Thomas Johnson - furnished with twoe cotes of plate and one Almon Rivet of the Townes (between 3 men) untrayned bills, Ashwell

1596

Mr. Capell and his servantes Barnard Johnson

1605

Henry Johnsunne, armed by the towne with corsletts. Wants girdell and hangers, tases and vambraces. Thunderidge

38. Burham on Crouch Essex t/s of parish registers at Society of Genealogists, London
(Marriages and Baptisms)

Mar: John Johnson mar Joahn (sic) Cramphorn 30 September 1594

Bap:
Johnson, Margerie and Annie, twins daughters of John Johnson January 12, 1583
Johnson, Mary, daughter of John, December 14, 1589
Johnson, Sara daughter of Henry, March 3, 1589/90
Johnson, John, son of Harrie April 25, 1592
Johnson, Mary, daughter of Thomas, November 9, 1595
Johnson, Janson, Joane, daughter of John, December 14, 1595
Jonson, Rebecca, daughter of Thomas February 12, 1597/8
Johnson, Rebecca, daughter of John March 18, 1598/9

39. Index of Persons, vol. 7 Exchequer Kings Remembrancers Certificates of Residence (for Johnson)

The Exchequer Kings Remembrancers Certificates of Residence is detailed by regnal years when known:

[all Johnson listed below]

James, Herts Hertford, James I
Robert, Essex, Elizabeth I
Thomas, Herts [period unrecorded]
Thomas, Herts [period unrecorded]
Thomas, Herts [period unrecorded]
William, Essex [period unrecorded]
William, Herts [period unrecorded]
William, Herts [period unrecorded]
William, Herts, 736 Charles I
William, Herts, Herts, 643 (Mdx Ossulston, Charles I)

40. Taxation Records before 1660

Records do exist at the Public Record Office at Kew, England for different types of tax, including documents relating to scutage (a feudal payment in lieu of knight service), poll taxes on land, lay subsidies, taxes on goods, taxes on aliens, forced loans, an abortive sheep tax, etc. The original records are mainly in Latin, some are damaged and the handwriting can be difficult to read.

41. Lay Subsidies (Taxes) after 1522

After 1522, a fresh attempt was made by the Crown to assess individual wealth, based on income from freehold land, the capital value of moveable goods and income from wages. In addition, local tax rates also were levied by each parish.

The level and kinds of taxation upon the citizenry of England may have been a significant factor in why people cames to the Massachusetts Bay Colony in the 1630s.

42. Bocking, Essex, England

Example #1:

Perhaps the examples within section # 42 are typical of *logical* assumptions made by amateur as well as professional genealogists about the ancestry of Captain John Johnson is revealed in the Parish records of St. Mary's Church, Bocking, Essex, England as well as civil records regarding Wills and Inventories.

Common naming practices of the Seventeenth Century was to name a first son after the paternal grandfather of the child. John Johnson's first male child was named Isaac Johnson. Thus, if John Johnson and Mary Heath used the common practice of naming the first male child after John Johnson's father, then an Isaac Johnson ought to be the name of John Johnson's father and a John Johnson ought to be Captain John Johnson's grandfather.

In the Parish records of Bocking, Essex, England, which is 33 miles from Ware, Hertfordshire, England listed is an Isaac Johnson born May 14, 1570 whose father was Johannis (Latin for "John" in the Sixteenth Century Parish records).

Several factors are instructive about this particular record:

1. The **naming pattern** *could* lead to (Captain) John Johnson and to his son, Isaac Johnson (i.e., Johannis (John), Isaac, John, Isaac)

2. The **birth date** May 14, 1570 of Isaac Johnson of Bocking, Essex *could* be old enough to be the father of Captain John Johnson, b. c. 1590-1593.

3. **county of Essex was the hotbed of Puritanism.**

4. The **distance of 33 miles between Bocking, Essex and Ware in Hertfordshire** is totally within the realm of possibility [for this record to be significant] in regard to travel and moving for work and marriage. Thompson, in *Mobility and Migration,* has provided many examples of distances between spouses of cross county marriages that were greater than three or four parishes and greater than thirty-three miles.

5. There were **others from Bocking, Essex** who emigrated to the Massachusetts Bay Colony in the 1630s.

Example #2:

Further, in the Admons Bonds and Inventories of the Deanery of Bocking (Index 1-45 of only pre-1700 Johnsons) is:

Arthur Johnson, clothier, Will and Inventory, dated 31 March 1642

Arthur Johnson of Bocking, clothier being sick...sons:

> John
> Edward
> Arthur
>
> Son John's wife, Mary, a warming pan
>
> Residue to son Bernard, the executor

Example #3:

> Susan Johnson, Bocking, Adm. 11 Jan 1676 #1076
> Inventory (widow)

The author hastens to **caution** future researchers that the information listed above in the *first example of Bocking*, while significant, does **NOT** prove that Isaac Johnson, was Captain John Johnson's father.

In the *second example of Bocking*, even though John Johnson had a wife named Mary, her death in 1629 in Ware, Herts preceded the execution of the Arthur Johnson Will. John Johnson did not name any of his children Arthur, Bernard, Edward.

Though John Johnson named one of his children, Susan Johnson, the Will date of 1676 for a Susan Johnson of Bocking in the *third Bocking example* is too late to be a mother of John Johnson of Roxbury.

There is no evidence that Arthur Johnson, clothier of Bocking and Susan Johnson were husband and wife.

But one can see in these three examples how errors are easily made in tracing one's genealogy. The three Bocking examples should not be used as fact in any speculation regarding the ancestry of John Johnson.

43. Genealogical records availability in England

Just prior to 1978, the "lost Parish records of Barnet and Kinxworth (1560-1692)" were found thus making the 'Allen Index' more complete. Possibly, additional records will surface and made part of existing records making such records more informative and useful to genealogists.

Because of the surfeit of Johnsons, and especially the excessive number of John Johnsons, pinpointing the actual ancestry of Captain John Johnson without the benefit of more identifiable information such as birth date, birthplace, baptismal date, or some reference to him in Ware or Great Amwell, his ancestry remains a mystery.

Until further records or references to John Johnson are found in counties of Hertfordshire and Essex, readers may have to be satisfied with the possibilities listed above.

The Public Record Office in England is in the process of developing an international catalog. Eventually, many of the records cited in this chapter as well as additional town and county records of all kinds will be able to be accessed by those who are   members of the Public Record Office and non-members as well.

Utilization of the Internet to access the international catalog should be a reality within the next five or six years.

CHAPTER NINE

THE GENEALOGY OF JOHN JOHNSON

To the extent that documents and records are available, the genealogy of John and Mary Heath Johnson is listed below. Abbreviations are used as follows:

> aft. – after
> b.= birth
> bef. = before
> bp. = baptized
> bur.=buried
> ca. = circa or about
> d. = died
> dau.= daughter
> m. = married
> MA = Massachusetts
>
> 1628/9 (as an example= means the difference between the Julian Calendar and Gregorian)

JOHN JOHNSON, b. ca. 1590 in _____, England, d. September 30, 1659, Roxbury, MA. Johnson, according to the Bostonian Society and Museum, Boston, Massachusetts and the City of Boston Cemetery Department, is buried in the Eliot Burying Ground *[originally, First Burying Place or Ground of Roxbury]* at the corner of Washington Street *[previously called "Roxbury Street"]* and Eustis Street located near the First Church of Roxbury, MA. His gravestone has long been gone.

[Note: Roxbury was incorporated as a town

September 28, 1630. Soon after its first settlement, the First Burying Place or Ground was established from the common land. The first tomb built in the ground was that of the Dudley family, before 1653. The second tomb was that of John Pierpont, before 1682. The third was the Parish or Eliot tomb, built in 1687. In the center of the ground are ten tombs: nine of these have horizontal monuments and one has a perpendicular monument. These are the oldest tombs in the ground. The first death recorded on the town records bears date of 1631, and was that of the wife of George Alcock whose maiden name was Hooker. The first mention in the records of the burying place was in 1641. The first plat plan of the ground was made in 1785, and the second in 1844. The plat of 1785 does not give the area of the ground in figures. The town of Roxbury records of May 18, 1785, in referring to this plat gives the area as three-fourths acre and twenty-eight rods. On the plat of 1844 the total area is given as three-fourths acre, two rods and fourteen feet. By reference to the outline plat of the burying ground made by order of the town in 1785, the original lines of the ground may be seen and compared with the plat of 1844, which shows the loss of the southern portion between the ditch and the line of the engine-house. All of the land south of the engine-house was conveyed by sale transactions by the town between 1785 and 1872. All of this land sold was full of the remains of the early settlers of Roxbury. It is believed that Captain John Johnson's grave was in the area that was sold by the town. He and his 2nd wife, Margery Johnson, are listed in the Annual Report of the Cemetery Department of the City of Boston for the Fiscal Year 1902-1903 as being buried in the cemetery.] [1]*

John Johnson was the son of _____ and _____
and was born in _____, England. John Johnson m. lst
Mary [3] Heath, dau. of William [2] Heath *(Edward [1])* and Agnes [2]
Cheney *(Robert [1] and Joan (Harrison) Cheney.* Mary Heath
Johnson died prior to May 15, 1629 and was buried on May 15,
1629 in the cemetery surrounding St. Mary the Virgin Church in
Ware, Hertfordshire, England.

John Johnson m. 2nd, Margery _____ perhaps in England just
prior to immigrating to America in 1630. Margery _____
and John Johnson did not have any children. She was buried in
Roxbury, MA in the First Burying Place now called, Eliot Burying
Ground, near the First Church of Roxbury on April 9, 1655.

> *[Note: During the year 1655 in the Massachusetts*
> *Bay Colony,many people died of an epidemic called*
> *the "cough." Probably the cough was what we now*
> *call the "whopping cough" or perhaps "the flu."*
> *However, the reason for the death of Margery*
> *(_____) Johnson is not recorded. Her death date*
> *may be only a coincidence that it was during the*
> *cough epidemic.]*

John Johnson m. 3rd, Grace Negus Fawer, a widow of Barnabus
Fawer of Dorchester, Massachusetts.

> *[Note: Grace came to America on May 27, 1634*
> *with her brother, Jonathan Negus. It is believed that*
> *Grace was bp. in Shelton, county of Bedford,*
> *England on January 5, 1603 Grace Negus Fawer*
> *and Barnabus [1] Fawer had one child, Abigail [2]*
> *Fawer who died before her mother married John*
> *Johnson. It is suggested that Grace Negus Fawer*
> *and John Johnson between April 9, 1655 following*
> *the death of Margery (_____) Johnson and*
> *October 14, 1656. Grace and John Johnson did not*
> *have any issue. Grace Negus Fawer Johnson d.*

December 19, 1671 in Roxbury, MA. She is not
listed as one who was buried in the Eliot Burying
Ground, Roxbury.]

Children of John [1] Johnson and Mary (Heath) Johnson, all born in England: [2,3,4]

i.   **MARY [2] JOHNSON**, bp. July 31, 1614, Ware, Hertfordshire,
      England. d. Rehoboth, MA. January 29, 1678/9. First m.
      Roger Mowry. He d. Providence, RI on January 5, 1666. She
      m. 2nd John Kingsley, March 16, 1673/4.

ii.   **ISAAC [2] JOHNSON**, bp. February 11, 1615, St. John the
      Baptist Church, Great Amwell, Hertfordshire, England. He d.
      December 19, 1675 during the famous Fort Narragansett
      Indian fight in Rhode Island. He m. Elizabeth [3] Porter,
      bp. February 10, 1610, Ware, Hertfordshire, England. She d.
      June 15, 1683, Roxbury, MA. Elizabeth [3] Porter was the dau.
      of Adrian [2] Porter and Elisabeth (Allott) Porter and the
      granddaughter of Robert [1] Porter and Margaret (Plomer)
      Porter of Landham, Essex and Watton-at-Stone, Ware,
      Hertfordshire, England in 1624.

iii. **JOHN [2] JOHNSON**, bp. April 5, 1618, St. John
      the Baptist Church, Great Amwell, Hertfordshire,
      England. He was buried July 8, 1627, St. Mary the
      Virgin Church, Ware, Hertfordshire, England.

iv.   **ELIZABETH [2] JOHNSON**, bp. August 22, 1619, St. John
      the Baptist Church, Great Amwell, Hertfordshire, England.
      She d. November 7, 1683 in Roxbury, MA. She m. Robert [2]
      Pepper on March 14, 1642. Robert [2] Pepper was the son of
      Richard [1] Pepper and Mary (_____) Pepper.

      [Note: The Pepper Genealogy lists the death of
      Elizabeth _____ Johnson Pepper as January 5, 1648
      but that would be impossible because her last child,

Jacob Pepper, was born on July 28, 1661.] [5]

Robert Pepper was buried in Roxbury, MA on May 8, 1684.

v. **HUMPHREY** [2] **JOHNSON**, bp. November 5, 1620, St. John the Baptist Church, Great Amwell, Hertfordshire, England. He d. July 24, 1692 in Hingham, MA. Married first, Ellen (Elinor) Cheney, March 20, 1641/2 in Roxbury, MA. Ellen Cheney Johnson d. September 28, 1678 and Humphrey Johnson m. 2nd, Abigail (Stanfield) May, widow of Samuel May, December 6, 1678.

vi. **JOSEPH** [2] **JOHNSON**, bp. April 20, 1622, St. John the Baptist Church, Great Amwell, Hertfordshire England. He was buried at St. Mary the Virgin Church in Ware, Hertfordshire, England May, 1622.

vii. **SUSAN** [2] **JOHNSON**, bp. July 16, 1623, St. John the Baptist Church, Great Amwell, Hertfordshire, England. She was buried August 15, 1629 at St. Mary the Virgin Church in Ware, Hertfordshire, England.

viii. **SARAH** [2] **JOHNSON**, bp. November 12, 1624, St. Mary the Virgin Church, Ware, Hertfordshire, England. She died before November 6, 1694. She m. first, Hugh Burt, ca. 1645. Hugh Burt died by August 8, 1650, Essex County, MA. She m. 2nd William Bartram c. 1653, Lynn, Essex, MA. because a dau. Mary Bartram, was b. April 6, 1654, Lynn, Essex, MA. Sarah Johnson Burt Bartram d. aft. April 10, 1688 but bef. November 6, 1694, Swansey, MA. when her inventory was taken

[Note: It is believed in William Bartram's Will dated April 10, 1688 and proved November 19, 1690, that the children named Bartram, namely, Mary, Elizabeth, Rebecca, Hester, Ellen, Hannah and Susannah were children of SARAH JOHNSON BARTRAM. Sarah Bartram is named as executrix of William Bartram's Will of 1688.]

In summary, Sarah Johnson married 1st Hugh Burt and had two children; Hugh Burt died. Sarah Johnson Burt then married 2nd William Bartram and had the seven children referenced above.

William Bartram died before November 19, 1690.

ix.   **JOSEPH** [2] **JOHNSON**, bp. March 6, 1627, St. Mary the Virgin Church, Ware, Hertfordshire, England. Buried March 30, 1627, St. Mary the Virgin Church, Ware, Hertfordshire, England.

> *[Note: Readers will notice two entries for Joseph Johnson. John and Mary (Heath) Johnson had two sons named Joseph. It was common in the Seventeenth Century to use a name again following the death of the first so-named person.]*

x.   **HANNAH** [2] **JOHNSON**, bp. March 23, 1627/8. Hannah Johnson is not listed in the records of Ware and Great Amwell, England nor in the Parish Register and Tithing Book of Rev.Thomas Hassell as having died in England.

> *[Note: Except for Hannah Johnson listed above, all of the baptism and death information came from the Parish Register and Tithing Book of Thomas Hassall of Amwell and the Ware Hertfordshire microfilms 991,303 and 991,326 of the Family History Library (LDS).* [6,7]*]*

> *[Note: It is assumed that Hannah Johnson died in New England prior to 1659 as in John Johnson's Will probated in 1659 following his death in Roxbury, Massachusetts only mentions five living named children who were: Mary Mowry, Isaac Johnson, Elizabeth Pepper, Humphrey Johnson, and Sarah Bartram.]*
> *[Note: There are some interesting discussions about*

Hannah Johnson in an article "William Bartram of Lynn and Swansea, Mass: How Many Wives?" by Helen S. Ullman in the <u>Essex Genealogist</u>, Volume VI, Number 4, dated November 1986. Further, there is speculation that Hannah Johnson was a "child who died young" in the <u>Ancestry of Emily Jane Angell</u> by Dean Crawford Smith and edited by Melinde Lutz Sanborn. There is no death listing for Hannah Johnson in the Vital Records of Roxbury for the period 1630-1700. Stephen M. Lawson, in his Internet account of the J. Johnson Family, believes that Hannah Johnson, instead of Sarah Johnson, her sister, married Hugh Burt. Obviously, additional research will be required before this genealogical riddle is resolved. [8,9]]

It was the intent of this book to list only the immediate descendants of John Johnson and his first wife, Mary (Heath) Johnson. Principal sources for the grandchildren and later generations of the descendants of Captain John Johnson and Mary (Heath) Johnson are:

<u>The Cheney Genealogy</u> by Charles H. Pope, 1897

<u>The John Mowry of Rhode Island Genealogy</u>, 1909

<u>The Pepper Genealogy</u> by Emily Clark Landon, 1932

<u>Certain Early Ancestors</u> by Cora Elizabeth Hahn Smith, 1943

<u>The Genealogy of Captain John Johnson of Roxbury, Mass.</u> by Paul Franklin Johnson, 1951

<u>Johnson Family</u> by Alonzo L. Johnson, 1971

<u>The Ancestors and Descendants of Ira Johnson and Abigail</u>

Forbush Johnson by Gerald Garth Johnson, 1983

One Line of the Descendants from John Johnson of Roxbury, Mass. to Lydia Stebbins by F.Z. Rossiter, 1907

The Ancestry of Emily Angell by Dean Crawford Smith, edited by Melinde Lutz Sanborn, 1992

J. Johnson Family (c) by Stephen M. Lawson (Internet web page; http//sml.simplenet.com/smlawson/johnsonj.htm), 1998

It should be pointed out that the earliest information about John Johnson and that of the first generation in America [his children] is the least accurate because of the lack of documentation. However, just considering the sources of information listed above, the descendants of Captain John Johnson and Mary (Heath) Johnson number in the thousands and thousands and are located in every state of the union as well as some foreign countries.

CHAPTER TEN

THE EDUCATION OF JOHN JOHNSON
AND HIS CHILDREN IN ENGLAND

As stated elsewhere in this biography, John Johnson could read and write. He dabbled in law; was a juror; and, was described by Captain Edward Johnson of Woburn [any relationship to John Johnson is unknown], as a "learned man." [1]

> [Note: Captain Edward Johnson of Woburn was appointed to be the Massachusetts Bay Colony's surveyor-General of the Arms and Ammunition in 1659 following the death Captain John Johnson.]

Evidence that John Johnson could read is revealed in a publication of the Collections of the Massachusetts Historical Society that included "*The Mather Papers*" in which there is a listing of books borrowed from John Johnson and William Parks of Roxbury by Richard Mather. The ninety books "borrowed of John Johnson and William Parks of Rocksbury the 10th day of the 11th Mon. 1647 In all 90 bookes pr. me Richard Mather" are listed below. [2] Approximately seventy percent of the male founders of New England could read and write, and one-third of the women.

> [Note: Perhaps Rev. Richard Mather of Toxteth, England who was the preacher at Dorchester, MA, 1631-1669. This Richard Mather was grandfather of the famous Rev. Cotton Mather who has been called "the last Puritan."]

> [Note: It is not stated who owned which books.]

107

_____ New Covenant. God's Allsuffic

_____ on Job

_____ on John

_____ on Isaiah

_____ on Opuscula: Ward, Sermons & Treatises

_____ Last pt of Warfare

_____ Second pt of Warfare

_____ Third pt of Warfare

Alsted Lexicon Theologicum

Ames, Rescriptio adversus

Assertion of Goum of ch: of Scotland

Ayry on the Phillippians

Babington's Works

Bayne, Helpe to Happinesse

Beard, Theater of God's Judgements

Benefield on Amos. 1

Bifield on the Creed

Bilson's Perpetuall Goumn etc.

Bradshaw on 2 Thessalonians

Bucan Institutions

Bunting Itenerarium

Bythner Manipulus Messie Magnae

Chemnitius Examen Concil: Trident

Crooke Guide to True

Blessednesse

Cyprian's Works

Dent on the Revelation

Dietericus Analysis Logica Evangeliorum, etc.

Dowman, Christian Warfare

Dowman on Hosea 1-3

Elton on the Colossains

Elton on Romans 7th

Elton on Romans 8th

Ferus Enanarrationes in Genesin

Ferus, Exegesis Romanes

Ferus on John: & 1 Epist.

Fox Eicasmi on Revelat:

Gerard Conquest of Temptations

Goodwin, synopsis Antiquitat

Greenhill on 5 chapter of Ezekiel

Gualther on the Acts

Harris Works

Hofmeister on Mark & Luke

J.D. Expositionof Lord's Prayer

Jo: Rodgers, Doctrine of Faith

Lewis, Right vse of Promises

Lord Supper

Luther on Galathians

Malcolumus on the Acts

Man's Vprightness

Marlorat on Esai

Moulin of Loue of God

Musculus, Commentary on Mathew

Musculus on Corinthians

Negus, Man's Active Obedience

Neh: Rogers on 2 Parables

Orsinus, Explicate: Catecheticae

Parre on Romans 8th – 16th

Peter Martyr on Judges

Practise of Christianity

Preseton, Faith and Loue

Preston, 4 Treatieses

Preston Remaynes

Preston Saints Qualification

Prick, Doctrine of Superiority and Subjection

Prideaux Orationos

Randall on Romans 8th 33 &c.

Rich: Preston of Sacrament of

Rogers on the Judges

Rollack de Vocatione Efficaci

Rollack in 1 Thessalonians

Salmons Sermon,

Ecclesiastes Culverwell of Faith

Sedgwick, Beariing & Burden of Spirit

Seneca his works

Sibbs Soules Conflict

Slater on 1. Thessalonians

Smyth on Hosea 6th

Stevartius Leodius in 2 Corinthians

Symonds Desertions

Taylor, Parable of the Sower

Taylor upon Titus

Theordoricus Analys: logica in Evangel: ps Hyemalis

Topsell on Ruth

Tossanus Pastor Evangelicus

Vdall on the Lamentations

Whateley, Carecloath

Winckelman on Small Prophets

Yates Arraigement of Hypocrites

Yates Modell of Divinity

In all 90 bookes pr. me Richard Mather

[Note: William Parks or Parke came in the "Lion" to the Massachusetts Bay Colony in 1631. He was a Representative in 1635 and for thirty-two various years afterwards, many of these years with John Johnson representing Roxbury, MA.]

[Note: Rev. Richard Mather was born in England in 1596. He married Catharine Hoult, or Holt, daughter of Edmund Hoult, September 29, 1624 in England. She died in 1665. He married second, Sarah Cotton, widow of Rev. John Cotton. Sarah Cotton's maiden name was Rossiter. Rev. Richard Mather was one of the first settlers of Dorchester, Massachusetts and its third minister.]

Assuming that John Johnson was between 1585-1592, his schooling would have taken place at the time of development of a system of grammar schools all over England, unless of course he had been educated at home. [3]

This emerging school system for the middle class paralleled the education system for the English Gentry class. John Johnson, was not, as far as it can be determined, a member of the class of power and privilege known as "gentlemen."

In the towns outside of London, there was a growing demand by Gentry and the middle class for a good education providing for suitable advancement to a college, profession, or those wanting to enter an apprenticeship. Yeoman farmers looked mainly to the school and the Church of England as a means of advancing their sons. While John Johnson was called a "yeoman," it is not clear whether his father was a yeoman also.

During the reign of Queen Elizabeth I, the House of Commons was overwhelmingly Puritan. However, the right or the license to teach in the schools of England was left to the Bishops by Queen Elizabeth based upon an old prerogative of the Roman Church.

Queen Elizabeth dissolved religious houses, charities and any connected Catholic schools during the first Parliament of her reign.

The Puritans had great interest in, and influence over, the education in the towns and villages. Coupled with the haste of Queen Elizabeth I to secure Protestantism, the schools began a shift from primarily religious instruction to English grammar, works of Castellion, Cordier, Latin, Greek, French and ciphering [math]. [4]

Likely, just prior to the birth of John Johnson, the Puritans in 1584 submitted a plan or program to Parliament in support of a "learned ministry' but also to support grammar schools and poor [not wealthy] scholars. [5]

By the close of the Sixteenth Century, the ordinary school student who did not have any command of Latin, had access to knowledge which had earlier been reserved for the Gentry class. Classics were translated into English and penmanship was provided by the use of 'copy books' whereby the students copied literature so as to practice their writing skills.

In the Seventeenth Century, many children began grammar school by the age of ten but some started earlier. If a student were going to go to a college, he would be admitted by the age of fifteen.

There was a grammar school or a chantry school for boys only [taught by a priest] in Ware, Hertfordshire, England called the Ware Free School that has been described as "carried on in the Town House." The school is listed as operating by 1612 [although it may have operated earlier than that] but it may have had its genesis at St. Mary the Virgin Church in Ware since it education was held in one of the buildings of the monastery in the Fourteenth and Fifteenth Centuries. Furthermore, St. Mary the Virgin Church was called a collegiate church by 1504 and had a college there in the 16th and 17th Centuries. Master Edward Haseley was dean of the college in the first recorded history [1504] of the college. American readers are reminded that "college-age" in England in the Seventeenth Century was 14-18 years of age. [6]

There was a girls' school at the School House, Amwell End commonly called the Ware Side School. This school is documented back to at least 1633 but may have been in operation sooner, and was used for the education of the poorest Ware Upland children to read and write. [7]   Whether Mary Johnson, b. 1614, or Elizabeth Johnson, b. 1619 attended the girls' school in Great Amwell before immigration to New England is unknown.   The females of this Johnson family might have attended a "dame" school but would not have attended earlier than 1620 as most education most likely would have taken place after the age of six but before age eight.

Attending a parish grammar school was not the only way a youngster could receive an education.   Home schooling, using textbooks especially written for that purpose, was fairly common during the Seventeenth Century. Since John Johnson could read and write, it is possible that he home schooled his children.

John Johnson's education and that of his sons could have been provided at a "petty" school according to Professor Roger F. Thompson of East Anglia University. In these last two settings, the "ABCs" would have been taught to the younger children, and some Latin to older male scholars.

The Emmanuel and Jesus Colleges at Cambridge University, Cambridge, England were explored since so many of the New England Puritans attended these two colleges.   Dr. Elisabeth Leedham-Green, Cambridge University Archivist for Manuscripts, has compared the handwriting of John Johnson to those of other John Johnsons who had matriculated covering the period from 1601 to 1629. The only one John Johnson she found whose handwriting was remotely similar to the sample the author sent to her was a John Johnson who was at Pembroke Hall from 1607/8 and graduated 1611/12.   Dr. Leedham-Green compared the handwriting from a 1622 Cambridge document of this 1611/12 John Johnson. She has indicated that it was "just possible that the 1622 hand *could* have evolved into the 1653 hand. But on close inspection there were a significant number of differences, the 1653 New England sample preserved a number of old-fashioned letter-forms (long 's', secretary 'c', 'd', and 'h'), which are largely absent from the Cambridge 1622 sample.

It is noted that the 1622 Pembroke Hall John Johnson signed his name "John Jonson" instead of John Johnson like in the New England documents. "Johnson" was the spelling used in all of the baptisms and deaths of his children in Great Amwell and Ware, England. The author believes that the Pembroke Hall "Jonson" and the New England John Johnson were two different people.

Captain John Johnson, however, is not listed in the Samuel Eliot Morison book, English University Men Who Emigrated to New England Before 1646 as one who had graduated from any English University or College.

The Artillery Garden of the Honourable Artillery Company of London, of which John Johnson was most likely a member in 1612, provided the art of shooting, ordinance, defense, engineering, and fortification.

It is believed that the Honourable Artillery Company of London provided John Johnson with the practical knowledge of defense, survival, civic duties, leadership, and engineering that he so ably used in Roxbury and the whole of the Massachusetts Bay Colony.

CHAPTER ELEVEN

THE CIVIC RESPONSIBILITIES OF
JOHN JOHNSON

Trying to separate the civic duties of John Johnson in Roxbury, Massachusetts Bay Colony, and the United Colonies is somewhat difficult, and maybe unnecessary. But it should be pointed out that in the theocracy of the Puritan Society, the Puritans did not distinguish between a "religious duties" versus "legal duties," "military duties" or even acts of friendship.   For the sake of this chapter, the author has attempted to show what John Johnson did for Roxbury; the military; the education of the youngsters; for the Massachusetts Bay Colony; for the United Colonies; and for others. Students of the Puritan period between 1550 and 1700 know that all things were done for the glory of God and for one's access to Heaven. Even when things did not work out, they were thought to be a "lesson from God." Puritans were "grateful" and indicated thankfulness to God for sending disasters such as fire, earthquates, floods as well as illnesses such as cancer, cough, 'brain disease" and other ailments.

The town records covering the period between 1630 and 1645 for Roxbury, Massachusetts were burned in the fire at John Johnson's house.   David Pulsifer completed the transcription of the available Roxbury records in 1861.   His copy of the reconstructed first volume covered the period from 1647 to 1730.   The activities of John Johnson prior to 1647 are based upon deed records, court records, and other genealogies.

D. Hamilton Hurd in the History of Essex County, Massachusetts, says that, "John Johnson was a learned and leading man in the colonies, and represented the town of Roxbury in the General Court for many years. He was also surveyor-general of the arms of the colonies." [1]

Captain Edward Johnson of Woburn claimed that "to write the history of John Johnson would fill a volume, and his worth as one of the founders of the government of the colonies of Massachusetts is too well-known to be recorded here." [2]

What follows is merely a sampling of the countless civic responsibilities of Captain John Johnson:

Roxbury

- Oversaw rates for cost of garrison for Roxbury
- Captain of Roxbury Military Company
- Selectman; elected numerous times
- Constructed fence for the "burying place"
- Helped select and buy a house for Rev. Danforth
- Helped re-write the town records
- Helped stake out the "highways" of Roxbury
- Inspected the two bridges in Roxbury
- Acted as arbitrator to settle disputes
- Was a juror
- Was a constable
- Established the Free School of Roxbury

Religious duties

- One of the Founders of the First Church of Roxbury
- Paid for repair of pound and clap boarding at the end of the Meeting House
- Established a rate [of tax] for repayering [repairing] the Meeting House in February , 1658

- Helped call Rev. John Eliot as pastor of the First Church of Roxbury

Massachusetts Bay Colony

- Set boundary between Charleston and Newton
- Surveyor-General of the Arms of the Colony
- Determined the boundary between Dorchester and Roxbury
- Deputy to the General Court; 1632-1638; 1641; 1642; 1644-1653; 1656-1659
- Surveyed boundaries between Roxbury and Boston
- Established boundaries between Roxbury and Dedham
- Keeper of the arms of relatives of Anne Hutchinson during her trial
- Put a cart bridge over Muddy River
- Confidant of Governor John Winthrop and Assistant Governor Thomas Dudley
- Served as Military Advisor

- United Colonies

- Met with Plymouth Colony to work out areas of defense, trade between Massachusetts Bay Colony and Plymouth Colony; trade with England; Indian problems

Military

- Clerk of Ancient and Honorable Artillery Company of Massachusetts
- Organized Roxbury Military Company
- Was Captain of the Roxbury Military Company

- Fought in several wars against the Native Americans

For others and himself

- Built a grist mill
- Ran a tavern
- Acted as attorney and power of attorney in many, many petitions to the General Court
- Performed scores and scores of estate inventories
- Was a farmer [yeoman]

John Johnson has been described as an enterprising soul because "being Captain of the Roxbury Train Band *and* a tavern keeper, he was able to turn an honest penny by establishing his headquarters on Training day at his own house, and thus combine business and pleasure." [3]   Because he was also the Constable of Roxbury, John Johnson had much to do with regulating the frequency of use and the conduct of the taverns in Roxbury including his own.

It is clear from the samples of John Johnson's civil, religious, and military responsibilities that he was a very responsible, trusted, and gifted member of the community of Roxbury and of the larger Massachusetts Bay Colony. As Breen and Foster said in their article, "Moving to the New World" in the William and Mary Quarterly, Third Series, Vol. XXX, No. 2, April 1973, ..."being respectable enough to be elected selectman, [was] a clear sign of status in any New England community." [4]

John Johnson was even more than just a selectman.

CHAPTER TWELVE

THE MILITARY HISTORY OF
JOHN JOHNSON

Thy right hand, O Lord, is become glorious in power,
Thy right hand, O Lord, has dashed in pieces the enemy.
Exodus 15 v 67

Honourable Artillery Company of London

Because of the types of responsibilities John Johnson assumed during the Winthrop Fleet trip across the Atlantic Ocean from England to Salem, Massachusetts in 1630, there has been interest in how John Johnson could have learned to be a quartermaster, a surveyor, a bridge builder, a road builder, and a keeper of the Massachusetts Bay Colony's arms and powder.

A visit to the Armoury House in London, England revealed that a John Johnson joined, by signing his name, the Honourable Artillery of London after April 21, 1612 but before 1613. [1]

Sally Hoffman, Archivist of the Honourable Artillery of London explained that membership in the Artillery was dependent upon a candidate for membership's ability to sign his own name. Unfortunately, the earliest original records of the Company were lost or destroyed during the English civil wars, together with most of the plates, and some were misappropriated by a treasurer of the Company. [2]   But a John Johnson is listed as a member in 1612. There were attempts to recover the missing records between 1658 and 1660 but the efforts were unsuccessful.

However, the Ancient Vellum Book is the oldest document in the

119

possession of the Honourable Artillery Company and consists of 165 parchment pages on which are inscribed three-hundred names of persons (including John Johnson) who were admitted between 1611 and 1682.

King Henry VIII chartered the Honourable Artillery Company on August 25, 1527 for the practice of military exercises and training, and for better "encrease of the defence of this Realme." Further, the King said, "Whereas we are informed that the worthie and commendable insitucon of yor voluntary Company of the Artillerie garden hath been soe well pursued by yor industrious and forward endeavors that you are not only become ready and skillful in the knowledge and use of arms and military discipline, but that, from thence as a fruitful Nursery, all the trayned bands of our Citie of London and the diverse of the Companyes of the counties adjoining have been supplyed with fitt and able Leaders and Officers whereby our service hath received much advantage and the kindome in genil a very great benefitt." [3]

In 1585, many gallant, active, and forward citizens enrolled themselves in the Honourable Artillery Company. They met every Thursday for practice in all aspects of war, and became so skilled that a number were appointed to command at Tilbury in 1588. The composition of the London Trained Bands continued to be augmented by those from surrounding counties until 1643.

The Honourable Artillery Company continues to be governed by numerous Royal Warrants issued by successive Kings and Queens upon coming to the throne. The Honourable Artillery Company of London is the second oldest chartered military organization in the world following the Swiss Guard at the Vatican in Rome.

> [Note: The Swiss Guard was founded in 1506 by Julius H. Della Rosa to protect the Pope's safety and his residence, watching over the entrance of the Vatican and keeping all unauthorized people out of the Pontifical State. The Swiss Guard is comprised of 100 men who are Roman Catholic, and have

completed basic military training in Switzerland. Members of the Swiss Guard must be under the age of 30, celibate, and irreproachable character.]

The Ancient and Honorable Artillery Company of Massachusetts

No regular military force had accompanied the Puritans to the Massachusetts Bay Colony in 1630. Because the initial towns were small and located several miles apart, the early communities found that they were dependent upon themselves for defense against the Native American Indians.

Regardless of the pious and conservative nature of the religion of the Puritans, killing Native American Indians became a necessity in order that the goal of establishing a "New Israel" in New England was possible. Furthermore, the Puritans believed that the Indians were less than human. Very few Massachusetts Puritans questioned whether it was unethical or immoral to take by charter or decree the lands that did not belong to them in the first place.

While by 1636 the Massachusetts Bay Colony of Dorchester, Charleston, Roxbury, Watertown, Newtown, Saugus, Ipswich, and Boston had what was called a "trainband," it was not until 1637 that the Colony as a whole petitioned Governor John Winthrop for a Charter for a unified military company. [4, 5] In both the London Military Company and the Massachusetts Bay Colony Military Company, the title of the organizations included the word "artillery." Actually, in the beginning of each of the units, the purpose was more for "military discipline" and "military strategy" than it was for muskets, powder and things "artillery." It was, however, a reality that weaponry was introduced as a means of defense.

The development of a system of defense was as much an expression of Puritan social ideas as were the New England town meetings and Congregational churches. The history of the village trainbands paralleled the development of other, more obviously Puritan institutions. [6] The organization of trainbands was a reflection of certain military reforms effected under Queen Elizabeth. The English trainbands were formed from able-bodied men drawn from the middle class. [7]

In New England, the town governments were involved directly in the militia organization. The towns were required to maintain a watch house, build facilities for the production of saltpeter, and to maintain a supply of powder and extra weapons. The Meeting House-Church served as the military armory.

Governor Winthrop denied the request for a Charter for a New England military organization in 1636. Winthrop wrote afterwards: ----"divers [sundry] gentlemen and others being joined in a military company, desired to be made a corporation, but the council considering from the example of Praetorian band among the Romans, and Templars in Europe, how dangerous it might be to erect a standing authority of military men, which might easily in time overthrow the civil power, [I] thought fit to stop it betimes; yet [later in 1638] were allowed to be a company but subordinate to all authority. " [8]

By 1638, continued uprising by the Native American Indians caused Governor Winthrop to change his mind about allowing the incorporation of the Military Company of Massachusetts now known as the Ancient and Honorable Artillery Company of Massachusetts.

Of the twenty-five founders of the Military Company of Massachusetts, several men had membership in the Honourable Artillery Company of London before immigrating to New England. Even with the scarcity of records, it is known that Robert Keayne, John Johnson, William Spencer, Robert Sedwick, John Underhill, Richard Morris, William Perkins, Richard Walker, and William Curtis were members in the old company in London. It was Robert Keayne who believed that a company should be formed which would be a "School for Officers and a Nursery for Soldiers in the

Massachusetts Bay Colony. [9]

John Johnson served as clerk of the Ancient and Honorable Artillery Company of Massachusetts from 1638 to 1646.

Isaac Johnson, son of John Johnson, was a Captain in the Ancient and Honorable Artillery Company of Massachusetts (1645) and Humphrey Johnson, another son of Captain John Johnson, was a Sergeant in his brother Isaac's local town military company. Humphrey Johnson was not a member of the Ancient and Honorable Artillery Company of Massachusetts as erroneously stated in the Paul Franklin Johnson Genealogy of Captain John Johnson of Roxbury, Mass. [10] Captain Isaac Johnson was killed in 1675 while storming the Narragansett Indian stronghold. [11] The Puritan military company destroyed the fierce tribe in the famous Fort Narragansett fight of December 19, 1675.

The Ancient and Honorable Artillery Company of Massachusetts maintains offices as well as a Colonial Period military library and museum in Faneuil Hall in Boston, Massachusetts.

Descendants of the original founders of the Ancient and Honorable Artillery Company of Massachusetts can join the organization as member by Right of Descent. Those desiring to affiliate with the Company may write to the organization in Boston, Massachusetts for additional information.

Roxbury Military Company

In a speech by the President (of the Massachusetts Historical Society), was read the following article, "The Early Militia System of Massachusetts" written by Ellery B. Crane:

"From the first inception of the American Colonies, through force of circumstances, the settlers had been compelled to be on the alert, and to hold themselves constantly in readiness to repel a foe;

and during a period of nearly two hundred years subsequent to the early settlement in New England, little time was given the settlers to rest from the preparation for, or the conduct of war. From the early records of Massachusetts we learn that all the inhabitants except magistrates and ministers, were obliged to furnish themselves with good and sufficient arms, as might be acceptable to the captains or other officers, and also to supply themselves with one pound of good powder, twenty bullets, and two fathoms of match. Each captain was ordered by the Court of Assistants to train his company on Saturday of every week; and these companies were styled Training Bands. About one-sixth of the settler's time was given to military training, and it was no wonder that after a few years such proficiency had been acquired in the handling of arms, and the disciplining of men, that the frequent company drills were discontinued, and once a month was found sufficient for the companies to meet.

The Clerks of companies (of which John Johnson was clerk of the Roxbury military company) in the various towns were required to make a list four times a year of all the male portion of the inhabitants in their respective districts from sixteen to sixty years of age; and all such persons, not otherwise exempt by law, were required to furnish themselves with one well-fixed firelock musket, with a barrel not less than 3 1/2 feet long, or other good firearm, a knapsack, a collar with twelve bandoleers or cartouch box, one pound of good powder, twenty bullets fitted to his gun, twelve flints, one good sword or cutlass, one worm and priming wire fit for his gun. Troopers were to provide themselves with one good horse fourteen hands high, a good saddle, bit, bridle, holsters, pictoral and a crupper. All companies were required to drill four days in each year. Fines for absence from drill were fixed at 10/ for each day missed." [12]

John Johnson was Captain of the Roxbury Military Company for several years. A listing of the men in his company follows: (from the <u>Winslow Papers</u>, Massachusetts Historical Society) [13]

Captain John Johnson	Joseph Foster
Lt. John Baller	Andrew Gardner
Lt. Eleazer Cawer	Eleazer Gilbert
George Allen	Robert Gilmore
George Allen [2nd Listing]	Phineas Graves
Richard Bartlett	William Graves
Elisha Bolton	Abner Hall
John Bolton	William Hooper
James Bradly	Joseph Keen
Caleb Brand	Benjamin Keene
Jonathan Brewer	Ebenezer Keene
Joseph Briant	Richard Killbourn
Benjamin Buton	John Love
Joseph Buttlers	Job Mohorton
Phineas Buttlers	Timothy Newton
Eliphalet Carry	Gideon Parkman
David Cobb	Elias Parmenter
Japhet Curtis	Simon Pratt
John Doty	Benjamin Price
Jonathan Dragon	Peter Reid
Obidiah Eady	Thomas Sears
Daniel Eavens	William Shappley
Jonathan Eavens	John Sturdevant
John Ferrel	John Thayer

Isaac Washbourn

Jacob Washbourn

Repheniath Witherrell

It is not known exactly when John Johnson was first a Captain of the Roxbury Military Company. It is suggested that since defense was necessary for Roxbury from the beginning of the town, John Johnson was most likely involved in 1630. The Massachusetts Bay Colony, however, did not have "national" protection of men from all towns of the Colony until 1638.

There is a court petition by the citizens of Roxbury in 1653 protesting the appointment of John Johnson as Captain of the Roxbury Military Company. During the 1650s men who thought the time for restricting train band elections had already arrived began pestering the General Court for reform. By 1656, the Massachusetts legislature responded to what it called the need for the "better ordering and settling" of the colony's military companies and ruled that henceforth only freemen, householders, and persons who had already taken the oath of fidelity could take part in the election of officers. This ordinance did not bring harmony to the village train bands, but it did represent a significant retreat from the inclusiveness of earlier decades. [14] It is not known whether the problems the Roxbury citizens had was part of the over all dissatisfaction of the Bay colony citizens or a result of a different generation that did not have the apparent harmony of Winthrop's generation. A summary of the citizen court petition is included in Chapter Seven as well as below.

The text of the petition of the citizens of Roxbury follows:

We your hombel petishoners, whose names here under are subscribed, hombly showeth that whereas the busines comfirming our elected Captain Johnson hath been contrary to our expectation presented to this honored Court, whether in a leagall way or illeagall way we leave it to the honored Court to judge now the busines being th[ese?], becaus at present we are unwilling to trouble the Court

with any seadious discourse, we are willing to cartifie the honored
Court that we remain unsattisfied with the choice, thare fore we
humbly [?reque]st this honored Court that the matter may cease
[   ] case your wisdome so cause for the [   ] of this
busines that then you would be pleased to give us an opportunity of
the Choise, which no way douting of this honered courts clemency
and troubling you, with any [?Sundry]   [   ] unsattisfaction,
but shal remaine yur hom [?ble]   [   ].
[Signed]:

Sargeant Riggs	Isack [torn]
James Bradish	
Sargeant Hemingway	Tobias [torn]
Thomas Weld	Richard ?Brad]ly
John [ ]	
Richard [Chad] Corprell	Edward Culver
John Baken	
Richard [ ]	Thomas Thorowgood
Henry Disborowe	Henry [ ]
Robert [ ]	William [ ]
Samuel Heminway	Richard Gardner
Thomas Hawley	Joshua Hewes
Jhon [ ]	Thomas
Peter [ ]	Joseph Wise
Richard Chamberlin	William [ ]
Philip [ ]	David
	John

Voted by the whole Court yt they see no Cause by what was
Alleadged by Sarjt. Ralph Heminway in ye maine of the peticon or
to alter or [   ] eade from theire former [   ]e or Confirmation
of Capt. Johnson at Roxbury. [Signed] Edward Rawson Secretary
[dated] 14 Sept. 1653

[Note: As in all documents of the Seventeenth Century, writers generally did not follow any spelling, grammar or punctuation guideline. Furthermore, copies of documents are photocopies of photos taken in the 1930's by the Massachusetts Historical Society. The copies are very difficult to read.]

Whether appointment of John Johnson as "Captain" of the Roxbury Military Company was yearly or for life is not known. Regardless, "Captain" remained Johnson's title in scores and scores of documents throughout his life.

CHAPTER THIRTEEN

RECORDS, DOCUMENTS, AND LETTERS RELATING TO JOHN JOHNSON AND HIS CIVIL, LEGAL, AND RELIGIOUS LIFE

The Massachusetts Archives, Suffolk County, MA Records, New England Historic Genealogical Society, Massachusetts Historical Society, and the University of Oregon Knight Memorial Library have been a treasure trove for recorded documents and records relating to John Johnson between the years 1630 and 1660. When it was possible to decipher the Seventeenth Century handwriting, the record or document is printed as fully as possible. Many records and documents were left in their original form, spelling, and punctuation. Some listings are abstracts of the actual documents.

Whereas this book is a biography and historical account of John Johnson and his times, the author has chosen to include some of the full texts of documents and records so that the reader can learn about the character of John Johnson as well as understand the historical significance of the affairs of the Puritan period. (In a strict genealogy, use of abstracts is more common than full-length documents.)

It will not take long for readers to conclude that John Johnson was a very responsible, loyal, God loving man who was a trusted member of the Puritan society.

John Johnson, himself, penned several of the documents and these are indicated with "written by John Johnson."

Sources for the documents are indicated as follows:

Cheney Family by Charles Pope (1897) = **POPE**

Dorchester Town Records=**HERITAGEBKS**

Journal of John Winthrop, 1630-1649=**Journal JW**

Letters from New England, ed. Everett Emerson= **LNE**
Massachusetts Archives = **MassArc**

Massachusetts Historical Society = **MHS**

New England Historic Genealogical Society Town Records
of Roxbury, MA, 1647 - 1730 (Roxbury TownRecords) =
NEHGS

Suffolk County Deeds and other Records = **SCR**

Suffolk County Wills (as published by:) = **GPC**

Records of the Court of Assistants of the Colony of the
Massachusetts Bay, 1630-1692 = **RCA**

Records of the Governor and Company of the
Massachusetts Bay in New England (William White Press)
= **RMB**

Commonly used Seventeenth Century words that today would be
considered misspelled are indicated below:

WORDS

accompt: accompaniment
acor: acre
agnt: against
alow: allow

alowed: allowed

armes: arms

barrell: barrel

bee: be

burnt: burned

clarke: clerk

collony: colony

corte: court

cruell: cruel

d: delivered

delivr: deliver

demaund: demand

fitt: fit

genal: general

genrall: general

howse: house

incuragmt: encouragement

invation: invasion

itt: it

Jo: John

Joh: John

keepe: keep

knwe: knew

Leift: Lieutenant

matrate: magistrate

meanes: means

mocons: motions

monyes: monies

m: month

nyne: nine

o: month

oune: one

per: person

peticons: petitions

psent: present

pt: part, point, portion

pvent: prevent

receaved: received

receit: receipt

recomdacon: recommendation

sd: said

shorte: short
suddaine: sudden
srveyor: surveyor
svant: servant
takeing: taking

Tho: Thomas
thinke: think
towne: town
toune: town

trewly: truly
vnder: under
wayes: ways
wch: which
whome: whom

wt: what

wth: with

ye: the

ym: them

yn: then

ys: this

Yt: that

viz: namely

&: et cetera, and

DOCUMENTS AND RECORDS

1630

14 July---John Winthrop to Emmanuel Downing

Brother Downing:

I pray pay to this bearer Mr. Edward Hopwood or his assignee the sum of four pounds, which is to be paid on the part of John Johnson for the passage of Wm. Timewell into England. I pray let it be paid upon sight hereof or within six days after.
So I rest.

       Your loving brother,
       Jo: Winthrop

Charlton in N: Eng:
July 14, 1630
[Endorsed Willm Timewell bill]   **(LNE)**

[Note: William Timewell was from Aldenham, Hertfordshire, England. There is no evidence in the Baptism, Marriage, or Burial Records of Aldenham that John Johnson's family was from Aldenham. How he knew William Timewell is unknown.]

[Note:This was John Winthrop's first communication back to England to his close friend and brother-in-law, Emmanuel Downing. Strictly a business matter, it reminds us that in addition to the letters that were sent *back to England, those returning brought news as well. The bearer of the letter was a servant of the wealthy backer of the company, Thomas Goffe. The man for whom Winthrop was acting as agent, **JOHN JOHNSON**, had come over*

133

with Winthrop. The original letter is Massachusetts Historical Society manuscript W.I. 81.]

15 September---John Johnson appointed to jury of inquest regarding the death of Austen Bratcher at Mr. Cradock's plantation. (**COA**)

19 October---For the establishinge of the government. It was propounded if it were not the best course that the freemen should have the power of chosing Assistants when tere are to be chosen, & the Assistants from amongst themselves to choose a Governor & Deputy Governor, who with the Assistants should have the power of making laws and chosing officers to execute the same. This was fully assented unto by the general vote of the people, & erection of hands.

Ralf Sprague is chosen constable of Charlton, John Johnson of Rocksbury, & John Page for Waterton, for thespace of one whole year, & after till new be chosen. (**RMB**)

1631

14 June---A Jury impanneld to inquire concerneing an accon of Battry complayned of by Thomas Dextor against Capt. Endicott. John Johnson and others were appointed. Jury findes for the plaintiffe and cesses for damages xl. (**COA**)

7 November---It is ordered that the difference betwixte CharlesTowne and Newe-Towne for ground shalbe referred to Mr. Mauicke Junr. Mr. Alcocke Mr. Turner & John Johnson to vewe the ground wood & meadowe, & soe to sett downe the bounds betwixte them. (**RCA**)

1632

7 August---It is agreed that there shalbe a sufficient cartbridge made in some convenient place over muddy riuer & another ouer Stony ryver, to be done att the charge of Boston & Rocksbury. Mr. Coddington Mr. Colbran & Mr. Samford are chosen to see it done for Boston, M. Tresr Jehu Burr & John Johnson for Rocksbury. **(RCA)**

4 March---John Johnson paid 20 Shillings toward the building of a sea fort to be used as a defense of the Massachusetts Bay Colony. **(RCA)**

> *[Note: This sea fort has been known as Castle Island.]*

1634

John Johnson was elected to serve as a deputy at the first General Court of the Colony in 1634. *[Note: He served for fifteen years thereafter.]* **(COA)**

14 May---First representatives of Massachusetts, in the same order as in the Record: "Mr. Goodwin, Mr. Spencer, Mr. Talcott, Mr. Feakes, Mr. Brown, Mr. Oldham, Mr. Beecher, Mr. Palmer, Robert Moulton; Mr. Coxeall, Edmond Qunsey, Capt. John Underhill; John Johnson, William Heath, Mr. Alcock; Mr. Israel Stoughton, William Felpes, George Hull; Capt. Turner, Mr. Willis, Mr. EdwardTomlins; Mr. Holgrave, Mr. Conant, Francis Weston. **(JournalJW)**

> *[Note: The names are listed by Governor John Winthrop without indication of rank or age of town. There were THREE representatives from each town instead of two. John Johnson, William Heath and*

135

1635

John Johnson commissioned to lay out the Cambridge - Watertown boundaries. **(MassArc)**

William Colbran, John Johnson and Abraham Palmer being appointed by the General Court to lay out the bounds betwixt Watertown and Newtown did make this return to the Court.

It is agreed by us whose names are now under written that the bound between Watertown and Newtown shall stand as they are already from Charles River to the Great freshe pond and from the tree marked by Watertown and New Towne on the south east syde of the pond over the pond to a white poplar tree on the northwest of the pond and from that tree up into the country northwest and by west upon a straight lyne by a merydian compass and further that Waterton shall have one hundred rodds in length above the Weire, & one hundred rodds beneath the weire in length and three score rodd in breadth beneath from the river on the southe side thereof, & all the rest of the ground on that syde the river to the lye to New Towne.

> (signed) William Colbran
> John Johnson
> Abraham Palmer   **(RCA)**

1639

John Johnson commissioned to decide the Boston - Roxbury boundaries.   **(MassArc)**

20 January---We whose names are underwritten having full

authority from ye Townes wherein we dwell to end all controversyes concerning ye Line of Partition betweene Boston and Rocksbury at muddy river concerning wch some doubt hath beene made, hav agreed yt ye Tree as [   ]e as they have beene marked by Capt. Gennison shall stand for parting Limits between both Townes and from thence to runne to ye Corner of Ded [ ] (probably Dedham intended) Lands next adjoyning, in witnesse of wch premises we have enterchangeably set to our hands this twentyth day of ye eleventh mo. Anno Dm. 1639

[Signed]

William Colbron p Boston	John Gore p Roxbury
William Tynge	Joseph Wild
Jacob Eliot	John Johnson
William Parke	**(MassArc)**

20 January---John Johnson again commissioned to decide the Cambridge - Watertown boundary. **(MassArc)**

20 January---John Johnson is by order of Court freed from training paying ten shillings p annum to the company. **(RCA)**

[Note: William Pynchon got himself into trouble with the Colonial Government for several reasons: (1) trading a gun for corn to the Indians in Connecticut, (2) putting the settlers along the Connecticut River in jeopardy with the Indians, (3) moving to Connecticut without permission of the government, (4) overcharging for corn from Connecticut that was sold by him to the Commonwealth of Massachusetts Bay thus making a profit which was forbidden at the time, and, (5) breaking the oath of a Magistrate. The General Court had a trial and he was found guilty. The statement cited below provides insight as to the

gravity of the situation for Mr. Pynchon. In the letter to the Elders of the Roxbury Church, John Johnson apparently had provided a letter of commission to Mr. Pynchon that Pynchon indicates a great sense of trust and respect for Johnson to represent him in Court.]

Statement

In the tyme of my tryall I was impleaded for unfaithfull dealing in the trade of corne, and mr Hooker was sent for by the Court to give his judgment whether I had not broken the oath of a magistrate and he delivered his judgment peremptorily that I had broken my oath but I being unsatified how he could mak his charge good have often caled up pon him to make it good and he hath often promised and yet delayed to doe it to this day: and yet the Elders of winsor [Windsor] Church have wrote to the Elders of Roxbery that mr Hooker hath acquainted them with it and therefore they must have mr Hookers challeng; and I conceive that the Elders of Roxbery will expect that as you have given them intelligence that I am charged by mr Hooker with this foule offence that either you will see mr hooker mak it good many wronges will follow. 1. His credit is wronged by vndertaking to mak that good which yet he hath not don in a long distance of time. 2ly [secondly]. I am wronoged in my Cause and made a grieved magistrate vnistly. And 3ly [thirdly] the general Court are wronged to ground their censure vppon his judgment. But I must ex;ect to see this Charge demonstrated by positive proofe, and not vppon surmises or prejudice or the like mistaken groundes, or els it is but a deceiving of the Court in their proceedings which is a dangerous thing to the Court as in the example of the ould and present misguiding the young prophet he trusted to his judgment and counsell but it cost him dere.

In another thing also I was charged with breach of oath as a magistrate for it was alledged against me (by mr Hooker as well as by others) that I should have bin so ready to further the Indians in transportation of their corne from woronoco that I should have but my Care which I manifested that I did offer to send the best I had and such a one as they like well of at another tyme. But because the Indian refused that and would only have a neighbors cano: I was charged that I ought to have borrowed it. Which gapped I also stopped and manifested that I intreted mr Moxon livine at the next door to borrow it. But the owner refused to lend it because notwithstanding his dayly need of it the Indians would not promise to bring it vp againe till fishing tyme, which ws about 6 weekes after: Then I was charged with neglect of my duty and breach of my oath because I did not presse the cano for the Indians vse: A strange reason to prove the breach of my oath: If magistrates in N.E. should *ex officio* practise such a power our mens proprieties, how long would Tyrany be kept out of our havitations: Truly the king might as legaly exact a loan *Ex officio* of his subjects by a distresse on mens proprieties (because he pleades as greate necessity) as to presse a Cano without a legall order. The lawes of England count it a tender thing to touch another mans propriety and therefore many have rather chosen to suffer as in a good cause then to yeeld their goods to the king *ex officio*: and to lose the liberty of an English subject in N.E. would bring woefull slaviryto our posterity: But which governments are ordered by the lawlesse law of discretion, that is transient in particular mens heades may be of dangerous consequence quickly if Mephibosbeth had but the lawes of an English subject to defend his right Siba could never have enjoyed 1/2 his bed. As though I am necessitated to speek much of this for my further clering in the breach of oath yet [illegible   ] may serve for a gentill caution to those whom it may conscerne.

I thinke it needful to put you in mind of one thing more: when I desire of you the dismission of my cause to the Church of Roxbury the Elders of that Church did write to the Elders of the Church of Roxbury. You allege this as one Reason why you could not dismisse it as mr Hooker.

Wm: Pynchon   **(MHS)**

[Note: See letter to the Elders of Roxbury Church below.]

23 March---Reverend and beloved my desyre and endvor with other godly persons among us hath bin continued longe for Church condition but kither to have bin lett, cherfuly but sinefull thinges have bin imputed to me, but I notwithstanding stand to defend my onocency in the thinges whereof I am accused therefore as duty bade me I mak bould to crave your advise and counsell in this case: the main matter is about faling from the Government of the River to the Bay Jurisdiction: my son Smyth is only calld by the Church to answer in this point, but one of the Elders tould me that this matter did cheifly conserne me, and also that it conscerned Mr. Moxon as much as my sonn, but they would choose to deale with my son in this matter but he was their member and therefore they had more power over him then over me, and in their determination they have concluded against us in generall as you may perceive by the coppie of it; now this is the point of counsell that I request at your hands, whether uppon scanning of all particulars you will judge me guilty of those sinefull imputations I would walk by consell and by my selfe by your judgment, for as yet the light of my conscience is much differieng from the churches determination, they determine many grosse sinns against us for doing that which we conceive we have don out of consceit of our duty: The particulars now sent by which you may judge in this case are these. I. The Churches determination: 2ly, my sons replie to the Churches determination. 3ly my sons letters to Mr. wareham a weeke before the determination. 4ly the manner of our joyning and faling from the River. 5 The coppie of the commission which brother **[John] Johnson** sent me from mr Nowell: by all those particulars I conceive you will have full light to judge whether you apprehended me guilty of those sinfull imputations: As for my sonns leaving the Church without leave: (tho it was when the Church was parted half in the River and half in the Bay) that is particular to him. But the point of Councill that I desyre is in the other things wherein I am a sharer. [in that letter we only rite such passages as the Church makes use of to prove our full dismission from the Bay, and we desyre the Court to expound their meaning in those passages, but you may see in my sonns answer to the Churches determination how

we understand and expound the meaning of those passages: but we cannot fully conclude that the court will make the same interpretations till we try their exposition. Neather can they conclud that their expositions are right till the minde of the Court be further tried.

For though I am not yet caled by the Church to answer, yet I expect to be shortly caled and therefore I desyer your advise is touching a letter to the generall court which is sent unsealed on purpose to intreat your advise whether you judge it every way covenient to be delivered in case there be a generall court atpresent: or whether your advise isto suppresse it for a tyme: I am intreated by the rest to intreat you to weigh circumstances of [   ] and mr Moxon hath writ to mr. Mather to helpe with his advise: but I leve that to you and if your advise be to deliver it to the Court then I conceive it meete that after you have given your advise so to doe that some other should take the letter and attend the Court for their answer and I know noe fitter then our brother **[John] Johnson**: and to him I have write that in case you advise to deliver it that he should attend the Courtes answer: and in case there be no generall Court till the Election Court then we conceive if your advise be not contrary to acquaint some of the Councill or the magistrates as you shall think fitt if possible you may set (?) any further light thereby to judge and advise what may be meete for me to do further in our case and how I may be able to answer the Church when I am caled: I am loth to troble you further and rest your brother in Christ [   ].

[Signed] W. Pynchon **(MHS)**

1641

19 January---John Johnson witnessed the will of Samuel Hagbourne **(SCR)**

10 March---John Johnson orders fence between Isaac Heath and Capt. Joseph Weld **(RCA)**

8 September---This corte, takeing into serious considration the psent danger of each plantation by the despate plots and conspiracies of the heathen, as also that they might bee furnished with such store of powder as may pvent any suddaine invation, have thought meete to appoint John Johnson, of Roxberry, the genrall surveyor of the armes, on the demaund of any siffucient inhabitant of each towne, to delivr the severall pportions of powder wch in their warrant from the Genrall Cort shalbee mentioned, according as is hearunder written & agreed upon, pvided the said inhavitant doth under his hand acknowledg the receit thereof, & securely keepe the same, not delivering any pte thereof out of the said store without psent necessity reauiring, & then on such good saisfaction as may most likely purchase powder againe; & if it bee not in such service used, the same to take into his possession againe, or such a full store of fresh powder in weight equalizing yt wch was delivred in place; and that the several townes wch have already had delivred any powder in their hands, wch sufficient pay, unto the said John Johnson, for that wch is delivered out, that so the country store may bee renewed against times of danger, & that the deputy of each towne, at the Genrall Cort of Election, from time to time shall certify the Cort of the case & condition of their said townes store of powder. Memorandu: That Hampton & Newberry had each of them a barrell before, wch they are to alow for, besides the barrell wch is now alowed to each of them by this order.

The Secretary, the Treasurer, & John Johnson are appointed to take account of Mr. Harvards amunition supplied to the countrey. **(RMB)**

9 December---John Johnson with others granted by John Stowe, all the house, barns, edifices, and all the lands in Roxbury and Scituate for payment of 200 Pounds of lawful money. **(SCR)**

9 December---Samuel Hofford having been much misuded by his Mr. Jonathan Wade hee is freed from the said Mr. Wade, & is put to John Johnson for three yeares, & to have 6 L wages p @, & for the

other 1 1/2 years it is referd to the court. **(RCA)**

9 December---John Johnson hath power to sue those that are defective about the countrey armes. **(RMB)**

9 December---Also, I John Johnson do upon my oath testify that about two years since I sold to the said John Sams and his heirs three Acres of meddow more or less and certain rods of ground adjoining thereunto, for Which I received in money fourteen pounds in full payment for the same, and I do disclaim to have any interest therein; The meddow and lands lying which in the bounds of Rocksbury in a place there called the fresh marsh. (Written by John Johnson) **(SCR)** (spelling and punctuation as in the original)

1643

John Johnson was a grantee to decide farms between Dedham and Sudbury. **(MassArc)**

7 March---To Richrd Davenport, Capt of the Fort of the Massachusets, at Castle Iland:

You are hereby authorished, & full power is given to you at any time, to require of John Johnson, surveyr genrall of ye countryes armes & amunition, all such armes & amunition as is allowed to you & ye garrison undr yor comaund, viz: for every souldier one sufficient musket, sword, rest, & pr of bandilers, wth 2 fathome of match for each musket; & for store for yor garrison one barrell of powdr, 200 weight of musket shott, 60 fathome of match; besides for evry 4 peeces of ordinance now in yor custody, or shall hereafter by ordr of this Cort be sent to you, one barrell of powder, 20 great shot, & 10 of match. A coppye of this order, by you signed, shall be a suffitient discharge to ye said John Johnson for his delivery of any such promises to you, you taking care thereof, & giving account therefore, according to the Cort order. **(RCA)**

22 July---John Johnson sold deed to Jacob Sheafe property he bought, to his son, Humphrey Johnson. **(SCR)**

7 September---It was ordered, Mr. Stoughton & John Johnson the surveyar should have warrant to deliver Capt Cooke, Leift Atherton, & Edward Johnson, or any of them, what they desire, as needfull for themselues or their company. **(RMB)**

5 October---John Johnson was ordered that he should take out of the cattle [fund] which came from Providence the money disbursed for that company, & undertaking, which is twenty five pounds three shillings & nine pence as per particulars. **(COA)**

17 October---John Johnson, the surveyar of the arms, was ordered to deliver two sacars to Mr. Robert Saltonstall, which Mr. Bellingham sould him, having brought them over upon his owne account. **(RMB)**

17 October---For appraising the cattle brought from Providence, the prisoners have liberty to name two, Robert Turner and the souldiers two, the Cort one; the prisoners refusing, the Cort, Robt Turnr, & x ers chose Mr. Colebron, John Johnson, & Willi: Parks. **(RCA)**

24 October---To the honored Court Assembled at Boston

Whereas it pleased this honored Court some three yeares synce to graunt unto your petitioners & dyverse others Certaine farmes and the place appointed where they shoulld lye wch was between Sudbury Dedham & Watertowne but for that the bownds of Dedham were not layed out therefore it pleased this court to deferre us by grauntinge them a time to lay out theire bounty; the sayd time being now past our humble petition is that this Court will now pleased to appoynt men to lay out our farmes according to theire former graunt

144

And your petitioners shall humbly pray etc.

Signed:		
	Thomas Dudley	416
	William Jenison	200
	Richard Brown	200
	Isaak Heath	256
	Joseph Weld	278
	Richard Parker	436 36
	John Johnson	100
	Josuah H[ ]ds	288
	Isaak Morrill	204
	William Park	181
	Thomas Bell	166
	Mr. Thomas Weld	353
	Philip Eliot	333
	Samuell Hays	177
	Gorg [George] Holmes	162
	John Gore	188
	Gorg [George] Alcok	242
	William Denison	267
	John Stow	253
	Mr. Robert Kane [Keane]	400

Dedham hay: 3 weeks further tyme graunted y'm [them] to setle their bounds and then Roxbury men to have ye Residue of their 4000 acres between Watertown Sudbury & Dedham if thereto be had & Capt. Keines 400 acres [ys?] it to be there also.

Also: the 3: farmes of Capt. Jenison Richard Brone & Jno. Johnson ar included in the same order, & Capt. Jenson & Mr. Oliver ar apoynted to lay out those farms: & to make report to the Court when they have don. (MassArc)

1645

14 May---The depts sent by each toune wthin this collony to attend ye buisnes of   this Courte are:

Roxbury: Jo: Johnson & Wm Parks.

Att ye mocon of John Johnson, gennerall srveyor of ye armes, his howse being lately burnt, some papers wch he was betrusted wth, of concernement to ye countrye, very hardly escaped, itt was ordered, yt a receipt he had vnder ye hands of Mr. Stephen Winthropp should be trewly coppyed out & recorded by the clarke of this house; wch is Receaved of Mr. John Johnson, srveyor, one bond of Capt Israell Stoughton, by sch he is indebted 248t; also, receaved a bill of exchange of Mr Edward Ting, of sixty three pounds, eight s., & nyne pence. **(RMB)**

14 May---Mr. Bartholmew, John Johnson, Left Sprauge, Mr. Winsley, & Mr. Hubbard are chosen a committee to consider of ye best wayes & meanes to destroy ye wolves wch are such ravenous cruell creatures, & daily vexatious to all ye inhabitants of ys collony, & psent their thoughts & conclusons thereabouts to this howse. **(RCA)**

16 June---John Johnson entered a petition to the Massachusetts General Court **(NEHGS)**

16 June---Mr. Shepheard, John Johnson & Capt Wiggin are chosen a committee to consider of ye lawe for ye disposing of inmates, & setling impotent aged psons, or vagrants, & either to rectifye it where it is defective, or drawe vp & pferr a bill yt may answer ye expectacon of each toune, & ye whole countrye, yt euy toune may knwe wt may be their oune burdens, & prvent multiplying of peticons to ys Courte hereabouts, & psent their thoughts herein to this howse. **(RMB)**

16 June---Mr. Speaker, Left Duncombe, & John Johnson are chosen a committee to joyne with some of ye magists to consider of such objections as will necessarily arise agnt ye last Cours order about ye Indian trade. **(RCA)**

16 June---Whereas ye some of fforty pounds was by this Courte given to John Johnson, generall srveyor, wth reference to ye service he hath donne for ye countrye seuerall yeeres past, & forasmuch as some pte of those monyes wch was assigned to him, (ye Treasurer hath receaved,) itt is therefore ordered, yt ye said John Johnson shall gather vp all those monyes formerly assigned him, (wch ye Treasurer hath not recd or disposed of,) & wt it shall fall shorte of ye 40 l he shall receave of ye Treasurer, provided yt he give in a just accompt ye next Court of whome & how much he hath receaved of those moneyes formerly assigned him. **(RCA)**

[undated, but must follow here]---We thinke it meete that this petition should be graunted. The house of deputyes doe concurr wth our honored magistrates in theire return to this peticon: And Doe desire yet Jno. Johnson may receave ye 40 L (according to his owne peticon & request) out of such debts wch he is privy to, yt are oweinge to ye Country wch are entrusted wth him by ye Country.

[Signed] Rob: Bridges **(MHS)**

16 June---To the Generall Court:
..........John   Johnson   of   ....of   the   ....such painfull.........places......otherwise were like to have beene lost, wherein hee hath spent much tyme to the loss and hindrance of his owne estate: for sch hee neither demaunded nor ever had any recompence, though others in that place who preceded him had good allowance and did very litle service for it., And whereas by God's providence upon the 26th day of ye first Month last past (March 26th) his house fell one fire noe man knowes by what meanes; and in respect of the powder of the Countries therein, they who came to quench the fire durst not doe what otherwise they

might would, both for saving the goods in the house (wch it is supposed might easily have beene doone), as also some eight other barnes, [?coe houses] & buildings neare to his dwelling house, being all his owne, all wch were Consumed by the fire, as were allsoe all his corne, about 20 bushels and the rest of his goods, except some apparell and other trifles.

It is Therfore desired by some (without the privity of the said John Johnson.) that the Court would in Justice for his service, consider of some equal recompence to be made him; that soe neither hee nor any other who shall succed him, may be discouradged from doeing the country future service.

The Assistants have noted that John Johnson shall have soe much delivered him out of the Treasury for his service as shall make upp twenty nobles formerly given him by the Court (wch yet hee never had) fforty pounds, whereunto they desire the deputyes to give their assent.

[Signed] Thomas Dudley, Governor. **(MHS)**

[Note: The following undated document may be an answer to the above Court petition]

We thinke it meete that this petition should be graunted. The house of deputyes does concur with our honoured Magistrates in their returne to this petition: And Doe desire yt John Johnson may receave ye 40 lb. (according to his owne ppeticon & request) out of just debts wch hee is privy to, yt are oweings to ye Country wch are entrusted wch him by ye Country.

[Signed] Robert Bridges

28 June---The Howse of Depts did voluntarily enter into an oath of God, verbatim to ye oath in ye Courte records, to deale vprightly in Himghm case, except Capt Keayne, Left Atherton, John Johnson, Tho: Lyne, & Wm Parkes, who did take their oathes in ys case before ye magists. **(RCA)**

1646

May--John Johnson appointed overseer of Estate of Joseph Weld; did an inventory of the Weld Estate proved December 4, 1646. **(GPC)**

6 May---John Johnson appointed to serve at this Gennrl Coute from Roxbury

7 October---Upon the petition of Capt Jeanison, Rich: Browne, Robrt Keayne, Richrd Parker, Eldr Heath, Leift Hewes, John Johnson, & othrs, for their land, formrly granted, between the lines of Dedham, Watertowne, & Sudberry, Mr. Aspinwall & George Munings are appointed to lay out ye same.

4 November---Edward Goffe, the serveyer genrall John Johnson, & Wil: Parks are appointed a committee to treate wth Mr. Sparhauke, or any othrs whome they thinke fitt, about such parcels of lands wch they, with Mr. Sheopard, Mr. Allen, & Mr. Eliot, shall conceive meete to purchase for ye incuragmt of ye Indians to live in an orderly way amongst us....

The petition of Misters Dingham & John Alcock is granted for ye division of ye houses & land, 2/3 to Jn Alcock and 1/3 to Samuell, according to ye division made by Capt Joseph Wed, John Johnson, & Thom: Lambe. **(RMB)**

4 November---Richard Redman, being indicted by ye grand jury, & tried by a petty jury, for being accessory to ye massacring of Luther, & fower more, in De La Ware Bay, by ye Indians, he was brought to ye barr, ye evidences brought & read before him, to all wch he pleaded not guilty, & was dischardged, paying a butt of sacke for his ransome from ye Indians. Contradicens to ys order, Edw. Rawson, Rob: Keayne, Jo: Johnson, and others. **(RMB)**

2 December---Dorchester

For the finall Determining and ending of all matters in controuersy: conserning the fence about the grett lotts, the capttins neck the 6 aker lotts and other prporsions of land now with the same fence: the proprietors who are owners of ther seuerall proporsions of land with in the sayd fence: haue refered them selfues to the Arbitration; of Mr. Isach Heath, **John Johnson**, and Wilyam parkes [Parks] of Rosbury; binding them selfes heerby to stand to what the sayd Arbitrators shall determine both in respect of what fense shall be mayd; and wher; and by whom, and euery won of the proprytors hath liberty if he please to fiue information in the case; to the said Arbitrators; when the shall com to Dorchester to be informed therin;

Richard Math	Nickolas Clap
John Gouer	Thomas millet
and 53 other men	**(HERITAGEBKS)**

23 December---Dorchester

Wee whose names are under written; being chosen by the inhabitants of Dorchester; to giue in ower determination about the fenses of a parsell of land caled the great lotts;......Wee make ownely this exceptione concerninge one parsel of this land caled pine neck if the owner or owners of that land or medow doe giue securyty vnto the aforesayde 7 men within 20 days after the date herof for euer to secure this filde from damage through any part of that land and also secure it selfe from any damage that may com to them by any cattel that have Right to feed in this filde that then this land shall be exempted from any part of this generall fence, otherwise to beare it proporsione Equale with other lands of like qualyty

> Isack Heath
> John Johnson (e)
> William Parke **(HERITAGEBKS)**

1647

6 May---John Johnson appointed as a deputy to the Gennerall Courte from Roxbury. **(RMB)**

6 May---John Johnson appointed by the Deputies to a committee to confer with the Magistrates about an order concerning the paying in of the rates to the Constables. **(MassArc)**

20 May---In ansr to ye peticon of ye wydoww Wilson, on ye retourne of ye committee, Mr. Colborne & John Johnson, the Courte found yt twenty three pounds, dew her. **(RCA)**

26 May---This Courte being deepely sencible of ye necessity of their vpholding, & all they cann to encrease all fortifficacons against forraigne enemyes, as also of ye great unsufferable pressures & extreame exigents of Capt Davenport, his garrison & family, (a thing no lesse greivous to ye Courte then burthensome to him,) & therefore thinke it very just & meete yt the capts peticon should be graunted for the three pticulers therein conteyned, & therefore doe order & enact, by ye authority of this Courte, that Leift Norton, Leift Johnson, & John Johnson, or any two of them, be appointed, authorized, & hereby enabled to examine the whole matter touching ye deffects of ye tounes, both in respect of arreares in payment & compleating of workes by them vndertaken, as also to levy all fines & penaltyes incurred by such neglect, & supply of amunition & such things as are wanting, as to them seemes meete & convenient; also hereby power is given to ye said Left Norton, & all, to levy all arreares afroesdaid by distresse of such inhavitants of ye said tounes from whom they are dew, or otherwise, & forthwth to pay it to ye said Capt Davenprt. **(RCA)**

27 October---Whereas there hath a long time bene a difference between Mr Robt Salstonstall, as agent for Sir Richrd Saltonstall,

151

& the towne of Watertowne, for & about certeine acres of medow, by him alleaged to be fifty acres, more or less, neere adjoying to ye towne, wch his fathr had possession of, for wch a tryall at ye Generall Corte now siting was to be had, & entered upon; but on a motion ye abovenamed Robt Saltonstall, on ye behalfe of himselfe, & for ye use of his fathr, Sr Richrd & John Sherman, as atturny for ye towne of Watertown, did mutually choose Mr Edwrd Carleton & Mr John Johnson as arbitrators to heare & determine all differrences betweene them in that respect, did & by these presents do, bind themselues each to other, in 500 l a peece, to stand unto, abide by & pforme ye finall award & determination of ye above mentioned arbitrators. Witnes now these psents, that we, Edw: Carlton & John Johnson, having heard & examined all ye evidences brought by eithr of them, wth relations to ye above mentioned medow, do give in this psent writing as or finall award & determination thereabout, wch we desire may be entered upon record.

In witnes to all ye above menconed conclusions & determinations, as or finall award concerning ye differences abovesaid, we have this 11th of ye 9th m, 1647, set to our handes. (signed by)

   Edward Carleton,
   John Johnson **(RMB)**

21 December---John Johnson was appointed to oversee the repair work on the Roxbury Meeting House **(NEHGS)**

1648

John Johnson was appointed on a committee to offer proposals to Commissioners of the United Colonies. **(MassArc)**

John Johnson signed along with Governor Winthrop, Thomas Dudley, deputy governor, Will. Hibens, Roberte Cayne, Humphery Atherton the following document:

To this wee reply though the present Commissioners whom we know well And whose wisdom and Integrity wee doe Not Question have declared theire tender care of an equall cource, betwene the twoe Colonyes accoding to their present aprehencion, of the case in question yet for as Much as wee canot foresee what commissioners may follow in time suceeding it canot bee expected that wee should yealde up any Lawefull Liberty god hath given us to the will and discresion of others, especialy such as see canot foresee whoe or what they may bee--2ndly the question of priority for possesion as well as priority of graunt must needs bee determined for us for the first possesion of Saybrooke forte, was tacken by Mr. John Wintherope November 1635 and of possion was before that, for those who went from Matertowne and Camberidg and Roxebery and Dorchester the sumer before tooke possesion in of name right and had a Comission of Government from us, and some ordinance for their defence, and in this state they remayned a good space --3dly if Mr. Pinchin were Now of hartford Jurisdiction as hee then supposed himselfe to bee might say still as hee did then ought to bee Subject to theire Impossisions.

Having thus Replyed to our breatherns answeres to our former Reasons againt the Imposson wee, desire the honored Comissioners for theire beter satisfaction, to consider what wee have further to propound Object against the saide Imposision and the order for the Establihing thereof

> *[Note: for complete text, see page 124,125, 126 in*
> *Records of the Colony of New Plymouth in New*
> *England, Vol. IX: Acts of the Commissioners of the*
> *United Colonies of New England, 1643-1651. David*
> *Pulsifer, editor. Published by Heritage Books, Inc.,*
> *Bowie, Maryland, 1998.]*

21 February---"It was voted that John Johnson [Edward] Deneson and John Gore wth Mr. John Alcocke ... William Cheney should be the men that shall ...ensuring year rate men according to theire estat...the defraying of ye fore sayd Charges of ye Ministry."
(POPE)

22 February---it is agreed with John Woody Constabel that the sayd John is to ffence in the buring plase [burying place] with affef [?] ston wall sefighattly [sufficently] don for strenk and workmanshipe, as allso to maik a doball gatt [gate] of 6 or 8 ffoot wid and to hinge it and to ffind all stuf and stons and work shipe and he is to iffinish id by the first of June next: and in "Considerashon of this work he is to have six pounds and he to paye him self out of the town Ratt [rate or tax] in wittnes we have here to sett to our hands the day above Ritten afore the setting here of the hands the penalty was putt att

Wittnese/s/vs::   /s/ me John Wooddey

                            /s/ me Joshua Hewes

John Stabenn   /s/ John Johnson

Beniamin Child   **(NEHGS)**

March---The Instructions wch this Corte giveth to you, John Johnson, Surveyor Gen John Johnson, Leift Josua Hewes, & Seieant James Olivr, Messingers to Shawna.

1. You shall first informe yorselues, & considr how the intruders into that place (& thereabouts) do stand affected in regard of the pticulers in this case mentioned, viz: whethr they do genrally incline to make satifaction, or to psist in maintaining what they have done, or whethr Weekes, or some pticuler psons, only do psist

2. That you demaund of them to expresse their answere by one or two, in the name of the rest.

3. That you be carfull to act ioyntly, that you may be able to give the fuller testimony about the pceedings on eithr part, & to take the Arnolds wih you, as you shall see occasion.

These instructions to be aded to the order of Corte. **(MassArc)**

March---The Massachusetts Bay Colony General Court sent Surveyor-General John Johnson, Lt. Joshua Hewes, and Sgt. James Oliver to warn the Gortonists again not to damage the Indians' crops. **(Journal JW)**

> *[Note: "Gortonists," so called after Samuel Gorton who did not believe in an organized ministry or priesthood. Instead, he felt that everyone should come to his own relationship with God. Additionally, Gorton saw no reason to listen to the colonial government, feeling that Rhode Island had no authority legally derived to deal with him. He believed that he was fit and able to govern himself and his family as any that were "then upon Rhode Island. Samuel Gorton and his followers were thrown out of Boston, and later thrown out of Plymouth, Portsmouth, and Aquidneck Island. He later migrated to Providence, RI.*
>
> *Oliver Payson Fuller, in his book, <u>The History of Rhode Island</u> (1875), wrote while comparing Gorton to Roger Williams: "Gorton was also a preacher and founder of a religious sect, and his views, both ecclesiastical and political, were not only obnoxious to the colonists of Massachusetts but also in a lesser degree to those of Providence and Aquidneck."]*

May---It is ordered, that whoever in this jurisdiction shall disburse money or other acceptable pay, for the repairing of the prison at Boston, shall be repaid out of their next country rate, with alowance of two shillings in the pound; and John Johnson and James Penn are hereby authorised to give receits to all such persons as shall so disburse, and to take care to improve the said disbursements, for the speedy repaire of the prison. **(RMB)**

2 May---John Johnson appointed Surveyor Gennll.

4 May---A letter from Springfield to John Johnson, surveyor gennull, referred to the consideracon of the committee, Capt Ting, Capt Keayne, Capt Hauthorne, Mr. Bradstreete, being about a bridge, rates, & imposts or custome, to Conecticott. **(RMB)**

10 May---The names of the Deputies sent from the several towns within this jurisdiction were as follows:

    Roxbury: Joh Johnson, Wm Parkes   **(RCA)**

13 May---The Governor, Depter Governor, Mr. Bellingham, Mr. Hibbens, Mr. Symons, Captain Hawthorne, Captain

Keayne, Captain Atherton, the Surveyor General (John Johnson), & Mr. Edward Jackson are appointed a committee to join the pursue the articles of confederation of the United Colonies, as also the acts which have past the commissioners already, which may seem to confound the power of our General Court, or so interfere with it as may in a short time prove, not only... but exceedingly uncomfortable... **(RMB)**

18 October---The lands formerly granted to Capt Keayne, (for himselfe & those who lands he purchased,) Mr. Rich: Browne, Mr Parker, Willi: Denison, Willi: Parke, & John Johnson, are ordered to be layed out in the place whereabouts the bridge should be built, over Ipswich Ryver, between Andover & Reding, they offering, at their owne charge, psently to build the bridge, if no farmes be layed out thereupon already; if there should, the country should be freed, & the own's of the land should be lyable to build the bridge. **(RCA)**

19 October---Itt is ordered, and hereby declared, that what agreement or contract soeuer the surveyor gennell, John Johnson, and James Penn shall make wth any marchant for the peuring of pouder to the valew of two hundred pounds, the Gennell Court shall

& will make it good in all pticulers. **(RCA)**

Itt is ordered, that the Treasurer pay, or cawse to be payd, the some of thirty two pounds ffouerteene shillings and two pence to John Johnson, surveyor genll, or James Penn, who are engaged for the payment of so much to the workemen that wrought at the prison, and this to be paid out of the first corne that is collected of the levy now dew. **(RCA)**

December 21---The same day it was voated that ye Meeting howse *[Note: in Roxbury]* should suddenly be sett in safe repair and ye Charges to be frayed out of ye Constables Rates John Johnson John Woody and John Ruggles being Overseers of ye worke. **(NEHGS)**

1649

20 August---John Johnson performed an inventory of the Estate of John Stonnard of Roxbury. **(GPC)**

20 August---John Johnson was an overseer to the will of Joseph Weld of Roxbury. **(SCR)**

1650

John Johnson, Surveyor General, sold 100 acres to Richard Parker. **(MassArc)**

2 February---John Johnson took inventory of the Estate of Lt. Col. Isreaell Stoughton **(GPC)**

22 May---John Johnson appointed as Deputy to the General Court

for Roxbury **(RCA)**

24 May---Whereas the Generall Court in answer to a petition [   ]
[   ] Capt. Robert Keayne Richard Broune of Water Towne and
Richard Parker of Boston ffor the laying out of their severall
porcons [i.e., portions] of land in such place as they should find out
did in yeere 1649 Graunt Comission to Mr. Edward Jackson to see
the same donne in the place in that order menconed next to Dedham
village as in ye order dated 23 October 1649 more amply appeareth
sch accordingly with Mr. Danforth a Supervesor of Cambridge they
have donne as hereunder written Apeareth under the said
Commissioners hand

Laid out unto Capt. Robert Keayne upon Pacussett hill beyond the
new village of Dedham and wthout the line thereof 1074 ackers of
meadow and upland being bounded by Mr. John Allens farme on
the south Charles river south and by East, East and North East, Mr.
Richard Brounes farme on the north and North west, Comon land
North and and by west, west and Northwest.

Ittm to Richard Parker [   ] being bounded by Mr. Richard
Broune on the South, Charles River South East, the upland on the
Riverett running into Charles River on the East and by South East
and NorEast Comon land west to continew so farr uppon the
Riverett taking in the meadow on both sides as [li] on the eastside
of the path: going from Pacussett to Naticke one hundred ackes
more added thereto by the Surveyor Danforth & sold to Mr. Parker
by John Johnson Surveyor generall In [   ] These severall prcells of
land wth Reference to the order of the generall Courte October 23
1649 I sawe laide [   ]. P [er] Edward Jackson

In answer to the Requests of the [   ] [   ] their severall portons
as above [   ] [   ] st to be Recorded in the generall Court
Records as they are laid out the deputies Approove thereof wth
Reference to the Consent of our honored Magistrates heereto: the
Just Right of any Judge [   ] any parte of this land alwayes
excepted. **(MHS)**

16 October---It is ordered by this Court & the authority hereof, that Mr Anthony Stoddard & the surueyor generall (John Johnson) shalbe, & hereby are, empowered to agree & compound with any man, or men, suffyeyently to amend & repayre the pson, & to doe whatsoeuer is requistie thereabout, and that paymt be made for what shalbe expended thereabouts, & in the effecting thereof, out of the country rate of Boston. **(RCA)**

16 October---John Johnson named as overseer of the will of Thomas Lamb of Roxbury. **(MassArc)**

16 October---John Johnson acknowledged by the Massachusetts General Court regarding his services as Surveyor-General and Keeper of the Arms. **(MHS)**

1651

7 May---At a Generall Courte of Election, held at Boston, the 7th of the 3d Moth, 1651: John Johnson was appointed Deputy to the General Court for Roxbury. **(RCA)**

22 May---Whereas, in the yeare 1644, there were lent by this Court two great guns vnto the owners of Mr Brtidcakes shippe, which, vppon a just value, appears to be worth thirteene pounds, which sd guns haue not hiterto ben returned, nor any thinge allowed in consideration thereof, this Court doth therefore order that the owners of the sad shipp, viz. Capt William Tynge, Capt Robert Keayne, & John Milam, them or either of them, shall stand oblidged to pay vnto the surveyor generall (John Johnson) or to Mr James Iliuer the sume of fifteene pounds, within fourteene dayes after the date hereof, in iron or otherwise, to them & either of theire satisfaction, for the vse & behoofe of the country. **(RMB)**

22 May---In answer to the petition of John Johnson and Wm Parkes, of Roxbury, ouerseers to the last will & testament of Capt Joseph Weld, late of Roxbury, afforesd, desireinge that the howse & lands, orchard, gardens, barnes, & eighteene acores of vpland & meddow to the same belongine, as it lyes scituate & beinge in Roxbury, may be confirmed to Anthony Stoddard & his heires foreuer, so as the said Anthony giues in securitie to the County Court now in adjournment, & to the sd ouerseers, to both their contents, to pay vnto Daniell, Sarah, & Mary, as they shall attayne vnto theire respectiue ages, the sume of fifty pounds apeece in current pay, or to the survivour or survivours of them the sume of one hundred & fifty pounds, keepinge them at his owne charge till they shall attayne theire respectiue ages; & in case all the sd children should dy before they come to age, then to pay what is justly due to them did they liue (by their fathers will & intent therein exprest, to the first siues children,) the Court thinkes meete to grant the petitionrs request, & doth confirm thesd howse & land to the sd Anthony Stoddard accordingly. **(RCA)**

14 October---This Court, takeinge notice of the contynuall paynes & faythfull endeavours of Mr Joh Johnson in the place of the surveyor generall, lookinge to the country armes, & peureinge many of the country debts, judge it meete he should haue due recompence, & doe therefore order, that he shalbe allowed fiue poundes p annum, & to begin from the time of the Courtes last allowance to him for his paynes in that imployment. **(RCA)**

14 October---John Johnson helps write the Book of Discipline for the Colony's Churches: Whereas this Court did, in the yeare 1646, giue encouragement for an assembly of the messengers of the churches in a synode, and did desire theire helpe to draw vpp a confession of the fayth & discipline of the churches, according to the word of God, which was psented to this Court, & comended to the seuerall churches, many of whom returned theire approbation & assent to the sd draught in generall, & diverse of the churches psented some objections & doubts agaynst some perticulers in the

sd draught, wherevppon, by order of this Court, the sd objections were commended to the consideracon of the elders, tobe cleared & remoued, who haue returned theire answer in writinge, which the Court, haivinge pvsed, doe thankfully acknowledge theire learned paynes therein, & account themselues called of God (especially at this time, when the thrth of Christ is so much opposed in the world) to giue theire testimony to the sd Booke of Discipline, that for the substance thereof it is that we have practised & doe beleeue. **(RCA)**

14 October---In answer to the petion of Dorothie Lamb, Elder Isaake Heath, & John Johnson, who haue sould a certayne pcell of land, contayning three quarters of an acor, pt meddow, pt vuland, vnto William Parkes, William Cheyney, Thomas Baker, & Mary Wooddy, this Court doth ratifie and confirme the sd sale, according to theire desires exprest in their petition. **(RMB)**

24 October---To the honoured Generall Court now Assembled at Boston, the humble Petition of Dorothie Lamb of Roxbury vid. [widow] & Elder Iassak Heath & John Johnson.

The widdow wth the overseers aforenamed of the last will of Thomas Lamb late of Roxbury deceased, having sould a small parcell of land part upland & part meadow conteining three quarters of an Acre more or lesse sometime belonging to the said Thomas Lamb & now sould unto William Parke William Cheiney Thomas Baker & Mary Woody ye late wife of John Woody deceased, Your petitioners humbly request this honoured Court to ratify & confirme the said sale.

The Magistrates graunt the petition & Request and Imp[rove?] therein accordingly if their bretheren the deputies Consent heereto.

[Signed] Edward Rawson Secretary.

The duputies Consent hereunto.

[Signed] William Torrey Cleric. **(MHS)**

30 October---The magistrates Cannot but take notice of the Continuall paynes and faithfull endeavors of Mr. John Johnson in the place of the Surveyor Generall looking to the Countries Armes and [?] curing many of the Countries debts and Judge meete he should be allowed ffive pounds per Annum for his paynes from the time of the Courts last Allowance to him and from this tyme forward tenn pounds per Annum for his paynes with Reference to the Consent of their bretheren the deputyes heereto.

[Signed] Edward Rawson, Secretary

The deputyes Consent that the Surveryor Generall should have allowed him five pounds per Annum from the time of the Courts last allowance, & from this time forward to allow him the sume of five pounds per annum for his paynes in that imployment with reference to the Consent of our honoured magistrates hereto.

[Signed] William Torrey, Cleric.

Consented by the magistrates.

[Signed] Edward Rawson, Secretary **(MassArc)**

[Note: John Johnson is called "Mr." in this document.]

9 November---John Johnson appointed to raise 50 pounds for the building or buying of a house for Mr. Danforth, Pastor of the Church of Christ in Roxbury.

A Levy made ye 11th 9th 1651 upoon all ye Inhabitants of Rocksberry by ye men appointed by ye sayd Inhabitants viz: John Johnson Phillip Elliot Deacon Parke, John Gore Robert Willias [Williams] and Griffin Crafts, for ye Raysing of ffifty pounds publiquely promised wth Joynt consent by them towards ye buylding or buying of an Howse for Mr. Danforth pastor of ye Church of Christ in Rocksberry. **(NEHGS)**

9 November---John Johnson grants, along with others, a parcel of marsh land in Roxbury "now being an island." Grants son, Isaac Johnson, 1/8th of marsh and creek. (John Johnson signed his name.) **(SCR)**

1652

John Johnson was paid 5 Pounds per year as Surveyor General for the Massachusetts Bay Colony. **(MassArc)**

22 January, 19 February---Know all men by these present that I Thomas Hawly of Roxbury with Doryty my wife for and in Consideracon of x pounds and fie shellings to us in hand payed by John Johnson of the same town have bargained and sold and by these present doe bargain and sell unto the sayd John Johnson one Ackre and one roode of land be the same more or les as it now lyeth north west upon whomlott [i.e., homelot] and meddow of the sayd John Johnson and upon the viz. South est lieing untio the water well lying north upon the [p-he] part of the whomlott of the sayd Hawly next his dwelling house this parsell of land as it is now lyes butted and bounded unto him and his airs for ever quitly [i.e., quietly] and pesably [i.e., peaceably] to injoy [?we] [ ] tising the sayd land against me the sayd Thomas Hawly and Doryty my wife and either of our airs for ever unto the sayd John Jonson and to his airs and assins [i.e., assigns] for ever. Witnes our hands and [seal?] s this 22 of January 1652.

> [Signed Thomas Hawley.
> Witness: William Parke
> [C in] [ ]

The abovenamed Dorothy Hawly hath released [   ] all title
and Claime hereunto of and in the [   ] bargained premisses.

[Signed] Dorrity Hawley the 19th day of ye 12 month 1652
before me Thomas Dudley, deputy Governor.   **(MHS)**

23 February---John Johnson concluded and ordered highways in
Roxbury to be set and staked out. **(NEHGS)**

23 February---John Johnson signed the report of a committee
concerning the rebuilding of the Castle and batteries on Castle
Island. **(MassArc)**

23 February---A John Johnson provided a deposition concerning the
brutal arrest of Archibald Henderson who was charged with
drunkenness; Henderson being dragged by the hair as if he were a
dog. **(MassArc)**

> *[Note: It is believed that the above deposition was
> by a different John Johnson inasmuch as the
> deposition cites the age of the John Johnson as
> "thirty-two or thereabouts."   This would make the
> John Johnson of the deposition born in 1620.]*

10 March---Dorchester

it is p'posed [proposed] to the towne [of Dorchester] about deliuing
[delivering] goodman Johnson [John Johnson] powder or giving
him a note. To p'sent [present] the returns of the p'rambulators to
the towne.   **(HERITAGEBKS)**

27 May---John Johnson was appointed to be a Selectman for the ensuing year **(NEHGS)**

16 October---John Johnson witness of a promissory note of Edward Burt, Charlestown, Hugh Burt [Sr.] of Lynn, and George Bunker of Charleston to William Park of Roxbury. **(NEHGS***)*

> *[Note: It has been thought that this Hugh Burt, Sr. of Lynn, MA was the father of Sarah Johnson's first husband, Hugh Burt, Junior. Sarah Johnson, daughter of John Johnson and Mary Heath Johnson, married Hugh Burt, Junior circa 1645.]*

16 October---John Johnson was deeded land in Roxbury by Thomas and Dorothy Hawley. **(MassArc)**

23 October---Itt is ordred, that Capt Lusher, Mr Jackson, the suveior generall (John Johnson), Wm Parkes, & Sargent Sherman, or any three of them, shalbe & hereby are impowered to lay out meet bounds for the Indian plantation at Naticke, betweene this & the next Court of Election, makeinge theire returne to the Court. **(RCA)**

17 November---John Johnson and others order new town records transcribed. **(NEHGS)**

[Note: The originals were burned in the fire at John Johnson's house in 1645.]

1653

15 August---A John Johnson received 5 Pounds from the Estate of Thomas Dudley and was named in the Dudley will as his "beloved friend." **(GPC)**

15 August---John Johnson took the inventory of the Estate of James Astod of Boston **(GPC)**

15 August---A verdict of jury in the Court of Assistants in a case between John Johnson, Roger Ludlow and Deacon Parks. **(MassArc)**

15 August---Magistrates
Reasons why we present the honoured Court with this Speciall verdict

Wee the Jurors of this present Court in the Case comitted unto us between Roger Ludlow Esquire Plaintiff. & Mr. Johnsons & Deacon Parkes Excecutors to Mr. Thomas Dudley Esquire Defendants in an action of the Case upon Account doe find that the Accompt have been this present Court presented unto the Plaintiff & that he had at any time liberty to search the Countrey Records: but not agreeing where the Costs of this present Court should be laid, we leave the Case to the determination of the honoured Magistrates.

[Signed] Joshua Scottow in the name of the Jurors.

Roger Ludlow plaintiff against Jno. Johnson & Deacon Parks Excutors of Mr. Thomas Dudley deceased defendants in an action of ye case upon account for 25 lbs. Delivered the said Thomas Dudley in the Adventure of the said Roger Ludlow in the joint stocke of the Company of Adventurors for New England. The Jury found that the plaintive had his liberty at any time to search the Country Records, wherein they found an account Rendered to the plaintive at the present Cort but not agreeing who should beare the charges of the Court they found a speciall verdict, the bench endorsed that both plaintive & defendants should each beare their owne charges.

Written in the margin:

Corte in England
Also the Court declared themselves that they thought it meet yt the plaintive should petition the Generall Court for sattisfacon in Law according to the agreement of ye Court in England in case he had not yet received it. **(MHS)**

[Note: Where abbreviated as Pl: or Plt:, the word, Plaintiff, was spelled out] . John Johnson was called "Mr." in this document.]

15 August---A petition of protest was received by the General Court by Roxbury citizens against the confirmation of John Johnson as Captain of Roxbury Military Company. **(MHS)**

14 September---To the honered Governor Deputy Governor the magestrates togither with the deputies now Assembled at Court in Boston

We your hombel petishoners, whose names here under are subscribed, hombly sheweth that whereas the busines confirming our elected captain Johnson hath been contrary to our expectation presented to this honered Court, whether in a leagall way or illeagall way we leave it to the honered Court to judg now the busines being th [ese?], because at present we are unwilling to trouble the court with any seadious discourse, we are willing to cartifie the honered court that we remain still unsattisfied with the choice, thare fore we hombly [?reques] st this honered court that the matter may [   ] [   ] case your wisdome so cause for the [   ] of this busines, that then you would be pleased to give us an opportunity to present to this honered Court our reasons and grounds of our unsattisfaction of the Choise, which no way douting of this honered courts clemency and Goodnes to obtaine, for the present we shal for [   ] troubling you, with any [?Sundry] unsattisfaction, but shal remaine your hom[ ] [   ].

    [Signed]:

Sargant Rigges	Isack [torn]
James Bradish	
Sargant Heminway	Tobias [ ]
Isack [ ]	
Thomas Weld	Richard [ ]y
John [ ]	
Richard [?Chad] Corprell	Edward Culver
John Baken	
Richard [ ]	Thomas
Thorowgood	
Henry Disborowe	Henry [ ]
Robert [ ]	Willia [ ]
Samuel Heminway	Richard Gardner
Thomas Hawley	Joshua Hewes
Jhon [ ]	[ ] Thomas
Peter [ ]	Joseph Wise
Richard Chamberlin	Willima [ ]
Philip [ ]	David [ ]
John [ ]	

Voted by the whole Court yt they see no Cause by what was Alleadged by Sarjt. Ralph Heminway in ye maine of the peticon or to alter or [   ]eade from theire former [   ]e or Confirmation of Capt. Johnson at Roxbury.

168

[Signed] Edward Rawson Secretary [on 14 Sept. 1653]
(**MassArc**) (**LXVII. 47**)

8 September---At the request of the military company of the towne of Roxbury, this Court doeth confirm Ensigne John Johnson to be their captayne, Sergeant Crafts for their leiut, & Seargeant Boles for their ensigne. (**RMB**)

8 September---John Johnson and others approved the transcript of the Town Records of Roxbury as a perfect transcript. (**NEHGS**)

1654

18 May---John Johnson took the inventory of the Estate of David Mattox of Roxbury. (**NEHGS**)

19 November---John Johnson chosen as a Selectman (**NEHGS**)

19 November---John Johnson received payment for a horse collar from the Estate of Robert Sharpe. (**GPC**)

1655

17 October---John Johnson awarded damages for someone's error in damming up the water for a corn mill and fulling mill. (**NEHGS**)

17 October---John Johnson witnessed the deed of Nathaniel Oliver. (**SCR**)

1656

19 January---John Johnson chosen to inspect bridges of the County of Suffolk. (NEHGS)

24 January---John Johnson, acting as attorney for Thomas Bell of London, passed a deed to Thomas Clarke on his behalf. (SCR)

24 January---A petition was entered by John Johnson on behalf of his wife, Grace Negus Fawer Johnson relating to her Estate from her former husband, Barnabas Fawer. (MassArc)

24 January---John Johnson of Roxbury, attorney [likely a power of attorney] for Mrs. Katherine Sumpter of London; held mortgage on a warehouse of Joshua Foote. (MassArc)

[Note: John Johnson wrote the following text and signed his name:]

"Whereas I John Johnson of Roxbery in the County of Suffolke in New England Attorney to Katherine Sumpter of Lambeth in the County of Surrey in old England Spinster as by hir letter of Atturney bearing date ye 25th of June 1652 may appeare acknowledge to haue reed of Left: Joshua Hewes of Boston in ye aforesaid County of Suffolke Atturney to the late Joshua Foote late. Late Citizen and Ironmonger of London on ye nineteenth day of September which was in ye yeare 1654 the some of Seventy foure pounds to shillings and Seven pence, & further doe acknowledge to haue receiued of Henry Shrimpton of Boston aforesaid & request of the aoue mentioned Joshua Hues Administrator to the estate of the late Joshua Foote, the some of sixty pounds eleven shillings and nine pence being in full satisfaction of the within written mortgage made by ye said Joshua Foote above mentioned of a certaine warehouse scuittuate in Boston afforesaid with the nailes and moulds within mentioned as in the which in written mortgage more

170

Amply appeareth, beareing date the 20th October 1653 to the aboue name John Johnson Atturney Atturney to the said Katherine Sumpner, weh said Mortgage was forfeited according to lae & by the order of the said County Court bearing date the 10th of November 1655 sometimes Respited &c as in yt odeer more Amply appeareth Now know all men by theise pnts yt I ye said John Johnson Atturney to ye said Katherine Sumpner to whome ye within written promises was made, doe for in Consideration of ye two aboue mentioned payments to me made by ye said Left: Joshua Hues for ye use of the said Katherine Sumpner, which I acknowledge to be in full satisfaction of the written mortgage in all respects, & doe yefore by these pnts Assigne sell and set over all my right title and Interest yt I haue of & Into ye said warehouse nailes and moulds in ye with in written Mortgage exprest to the said Joshua Hues late Atturney & now Administrator to the Estate of said Joshua Foote, or yt I had might, or any way ought to haue yrin, & doe hereby fully discharge, the said Joshua Hues Atturney & Administrator to ye said Joshua Foote, off & fro all & all manner of debts dues accompts, bonds bills, Mortgages judgements executions & engagements whatsoeuer heretofore any way due oweing or belinging to the said Joshua Foote to haue payd unto the said Katherine Sumpner, hir executors Administrators or assignes In witnes whereof I haue this twenty fourth of March 1656 set to my hand and seale.

John Johnson & a seale   **(SCR)**

24 January---Agreement of the will of Barnabas Fawer, John Johnson's wife's former husband was confirmed. **(MassArc)**

13 July---Bond established for John Johnson for appearance in Court, **(MHS)**

13 July---John Johnson took inventory of the Estate of John Burrell. **(NEHGS)**

1657

John Johnson was attorney for William Sheldon vs. Administrators of the Estate of Joshua Foote. Court voted in favor. **(MassArc)**

John Johnson given power of attorney by Jacob Sheafe to collect the sum due William Sheldon of London from the Estate of Joshua Foote. **(MassArc)**

6 May---Mr. John Johnson having bin long serviceable to the country in the place of surveyor genll, for which he hath never had any satisfaction, which this Court considering off, thinkes meet to graunt him 300 acors, in any place where he can find it, according to law. **(RCA)**

1658

12 January---We John Johnson Isaack Moril Ed Denison & Peleg Heath hauing upon the twenty therd of April uewed the place & lane doe ioyntly aprouse the granting liberty to Griffin Crafts for what is aboue desired by him. Witnesse our hands

    Ed: Denison   John Johnson Isack Morrell Peleg Heath
(NEHGS)

7 July---John Johnson deposed that he saw John Dane sign and publish his last will. **(SCR)**

20 May---John Johnson, Surveyor General; copy of grant of land and a Bill of sale to William Park. **(MassArc)**

[Memorandum?] John Johnson of Roxbury having bin longe sericeable to the Country in the place of Surveyor Gen'll. For which he hath never had any Satisfaction in which this Courte conserning off thinkes meet to graunt him three hundred Acres of Land in any place where he can find it according to law.

This is a True Coppie of the Courts graunt in Anno 57 as Attests William Torrey Cleric.

John Johnson doe acknowledge that [   ] of William Park [   ] the day of the [   ] three hundred Acres of land and the sayd Park and his heires for ever [   ] [   ] this 19 day of june 1658.

        [Signed] John Johnson

10 August---This is to Certify to all whomsoever It may Concern more especially the Honnored Generall Court of the Massachusetts that I John Johnson Surveyor Generall doe hereby Acknowledge to have Receaved into my hands for ye use of the Jurisdiction of the Massachusetts two barrells of Good Powder of Mr. Henry Shrimpton by order from Edward Rawson Secretary to ye Jurisdiction aforesaid and it yt wch Capt. Bond was to pay as a fine for bringing in Quakers into this Jurisdiction. In Wittnes where of I have subscribed my name this 10th of August 1658.

        [Signed] By me John Johnson

        Witness John ffirnside [Fireside]

10 August---John Johnson petitioned that the fine of Richard Sutton of the same town, be remitted. (MassArc)

1659

John Johnson signed receipt for two barrels of powder for the country's use. (MassArc)

30 January---The same day for stakeing out at the hie wayes in the Towne of Roxbury thare ware men chosen and fully impowered by the Towne to stake them out and settel al matters consarning he wayes as thay are at first for breadth apointed by the Towne act the men chose ware namly as followeth theas men haue also liberty to chose one man man or more to giue them light conserning any of the hie wayes and those men thus chosen or hired by them to be paid for such day or dayes as thay may make vse of them, (out of the Towne Rate)

> Robt: Willyams: Edw: Riggs Will: parks: Isack: Morell Edw: Denison: John Rugles Sr Capt: Johnson: Edw: Bridge John: Weld: Peleg: Heath
> John Johnson, as Commissioner, heard complaint by John Rugles, Jr. against Peleg Heath and Isaac Heath about a "highway" for carting through his land. **(NEHGS)**

1660

Reference is made to John Johnson, deceased, Attorney for Katherine Sumpter regarding the receipt of 20 sets of molds and eight thousand four hundred nails by John Johnson. Eleven shilling and nine pence (00.11.09) had been paid to John Johnson prior to his death. A Deed. **(SCR)**

CHAPTER FOURTEEN

DESCRIPTION OF REAL PROPERTY OWNED BY JOHN JOHNSON AND THE GREAT FIRE OF JOHN JOHNSON'S HOME IN 1645

A disaster befell the Johnson household on April 6, 1645 when a fire leveled the house and other outbuildings as well as the powder for the Massachusetts Bay Colony's defense.

There are several accounts of the fire and explosion. The Governor John Winthrop account, which follows in the <u>Winthrop's Journal,</u> 1630 - 1649 as published by Charles Scribner's Sons, New York, is the most descriptive.

> "Two great fires happened this week, one at Salem; Mr. Downing having built a new house at his farm, he being gone to England, and his wife and family gone to the church meeting upon the Lord's day, the chimney took fire, and burnt down the house, and bedding, apparel, and household to the value of 200 pounds. The other was at Roxbury this day. John Johnson, the surveyor general of the ammunition, a very industrious and faithful man in his place, having built a fair house in the midst of the town, with diverse barns and other out houses, it fell on fire in the day time, (no man knowing by what occasion,) and there being in it seventeen barrels of the country's powder and many arms, all was suddenly burnt and blown up, to the value of 4 or 500 pounds, wherein a special providence of God appeared, for he being from home, the people came together to help, and many were in the house, no man thinking of the powder, till one of the company put them in mind of it, whereupon they all withdrew, and soon

after the powder took fire, and blew up all about it, and shook the houses in Boston and Cambridge,so as men thought it has been an earthquake, and carried great pieces of timber a great way off and some rags and such light things beyond Boston meeting house. There being then a stiff gale at south, it drove the fire from the other houses in the town, (for this was the most northerly,) otherwise it had endangered the greatest part of the town. This loss of our powder was the more observable in two respects, 1. because the court had not taken that care they ought to pay for it, having been owing for diverse years; 2. In that, at the court be-fore, they had refused to help our countrymen in Virginia, who had written to us for some for the defense against the Indians, and also to help our brethren of Plymouth in their want." [1]

It is no surprise that the "men" of the Colony thought it was an earthquake. The Massachusetts Bay area had experienced two earthquakes: one in 1638 and another in January of 1639 where it lasted from the first of January to the fourth of January and was "more generally felt, and the same noise heard in many places." [2]

It is believed that the Winthrop description of the fire and explosion of the house and outbuildings of John Johnson in Roxbury leaves no doubt that he had to replace everything: house, household goods, apparel, outbuildings. This account of the fire makes the Will of John Johnson in 1659 more significant because that which is listed in the Will was a replacement of all of his worldly goods.

Unfortunately, the Roxbury Town records, the military records, First Church of Roxbury records from the period between 1630 to 1645, and any personal information about John Johnson and his family was destroyed in this tragic fire.

However, there is an account of the real property owned by John

Johnson in February 1654 from the *Book of Possessions in Roxbury* Published by the Boston Records Commissioners as City Document No. 114 in 1884 from reconstructed Roxbury Town Records and approved by John Johnson and others in 1654:

"John Johnson his house, barne, and hous lott on the back side of his orchyard and buildings lying together with liberty to inclose the swamp and brooke before the same, not anoying any highway, conteining in all eight accres more or lesse, upon Thomas Lambs heires towards the west, and upon william Denison east. And twenty accres more or lesse of mowing ground upon the march of Mr. Thomas Weld, and the land of Thomas Lamb on the east and so compassed with muddy riuer and stoney riuer, and ten accres of woodland more or lesse lying tetweene the great lotts and the lands of the heires of Samuell Hagborne, and so turning up betweene the lott lately bought of George Bowers and a way leading to Rocky swamp. And doure accres more or lesse lying betweene the way leading to Rocky swamp Northweast last deuission, in the first and third deuission being the fourth lott their one hundred ten (the nearest halfe of this hundred and ten accres in sold by John Johnson to Griffin Craft) accres and one quarter. And one and fifty accres and halfe bought of Edward Porter and John Pettit lying in the thousand accres at Deddam. And six accres more or less bought of Jeames Morgan, upon stoney riuer west. And upon a highway leading to the great pond east. And sixteene accres and a halfe more or lesse bought of Richard Goad lying at rocky swamp, abutting upon the land of Edward Pason west, and upon the land of Edward Bridges east. And an accre and a quarter more or lesse, lately the land of Thomas Lamb, upon the home lott and Meadow of John Johnson Northwest.

Upon the highway leading to the matermill southeast. And three accres of woodland more or lesse lately the land of John Stebbins, lying at Rocky swamp. And fower accres of fresh meadow more or lesse lately bought of John Parepoynt lying in the great meades betweene the lands of Isaack Morrill nad William Cheiney. And thirteene accres and twenty rod of land wood and pasture bought of Thomas Gardner in the nookes next Dorchester, betweene the lands of Henry Farnham and the lands of the heires of Thomas Stannard."

CHAPTER FIFTEEN

THE WILL OF JOHN JOHNSON
OF ROXBURY

Examining the wills of the Seventeenth Century tells a lot about the person. For example, a listing of books could indicate that the deceased could read; assets of hundreds of acres could indicate wealth. Furthermore, inventory of a deceased persons clothing or jewelry or household goods could be a clue to the status or rank of a person.

In the case of Captain John Johnson, there is a listing of clothing worth L 20. This valuation of his clothing would be quite high for the times in 1659. Moreover, the fact that he had carpets might indicate that he had more wealth than others. Since his house burned to the ground in 1645, it is not likely that John Johnson brought the carpets with him in the Arbella but purchased it from England or elsewhere later. The inventory also lists silver spoons and other items, which were uncommon to a person of Captain Johnson's social standing yet a sign of wealth and dignity. The fact that there are books and a Bible listed would lead one to understand that Captain John Johnson could read. [We know that he could write. See the Chapter Seven.]

Listed below is the complete will of Captain John Johnson who died September 30, 1659 in Roxbury, Massachusetts.

The Complete Will and Inventory of Captain John Johnson [1]

"The last will & Testament of John Johnson of Roxbury this 30t of the 7t 59 having my perfect memory & understanding by the blessing of my mercyfull Father, whose reconciled face in Jesus shrift my Soule waiteth to behould I dispose of my worldly goods & estate as followeth. My dwelling house & certaine lands I have allready given to my beloved wife during the terme of her natural life according to a deed wch [meaning which] is extant wch deede my will is shall be fullfilled, wherin also I have given her 60 li for her houshold furniture wch house and lands, after my wives decease I give unto my 5 children to be equally divided, my eldest Sonne [Isaac] having a double portion therin, according to the word of God.

I give unto my two grandchildren who have lived with me, Elizabeth Johnson & Mehittabel Johnson, each of them 5li this to be paide them one yeare after my decease. I have formerly given to my Soones Isaak Johnson & Robert Pepper [actually a son-in-law] a parcel of lands of 55 acres in the third division of the Towne [Roxbury], wch I doe hereby confirme.

All the rest of my lands debts & moveable goods, my debts & funeral charges being first discharged, I doe give unto my five children to be equally divided, my eldest Sonne having a double portion.

Also I make my Sonns Isaak Johnson & Robert Pepper my executors of this my last will & Testament & I request my dear brethren Elder Heath and Deakon Park, to be overseers of this my will & Testament & in token of my love I give ym [probably "them"] 40s.

If my children should disagree in any thing I doe order them to choose one man more, to these my overseers, & stand to theire determination.

witness   the mark of John Johnson
John Eliot

John Alcoke and Edward Denison deposed 15 October 1659 that they were present when John Johnson signed his will.

[Note: While John Johnson "made a mark" in place of a signature on his will, it is well established in the Records and Documents Relating to John Johnson Chapter that John Johnson could write. It might be best explained that John Johnson was near death and unable to use a pen to sign his name.]

Inventory

An Inventorie of goods and Chattell of John Johnson Late of Roxbury Desesed

[value given in Pounds. Shillings. Pence]

Imprimis 2 fether beds 2 bolsters, 3 pilows 2 sheets 3 blankets and A rugg with curtains and valenss with a bedsteed	10.00.00
1 tabl 6 joyn stools and a carpet	2.00.00
10 cuishons 2 blanckets and a rug	2.16.00
6 chairs 2 small Joyne stools	00.15.00
A liverey cuberd with a cloath & cuishon	01.06.08
2 cobirons an Iron and fyre shovell and tongs & bellowes	00.13.00
1 drincking glass 1 houre glass	00.01.06
3 hats & wering Aparell with boots stockings bands, caps hand churches	20.00.00
2 bibls 1 psalme booke and 8 books more	01.05.00
12lb of yearn 13 scains	01.04.00
1 curtain rod 1 pair of pinsers 2 pair of sheers	00.03.06
8 silver spoons	02.00.00
1 yard of linen cloth 1 box with 2 pair of sisers with sum other small things	00.03.00
1 box with spice	00.02.00
1 bed steed with 1 fether bed & 1 flock bed & 4 pillows 1 ould & bolster	

with a quilt & a rugg	06.10.00
2 pair of sheets 26 napkins 4 pillowbers	
1 cuberd cloath 2 table cloaths with 1 box	03.14.00
4 pillow beers 1 table cloath 6 paire of shaets	05.16.00
3 fruit dishes of earth [pottery]	00.01.06
1 yard 1/2 of broad cloath	01.00.00
in red shagg bayes 3 yards ¼	00.10.00
allmost 8 yards of searge	02.02.00
11 yards of stufe at 3s for yard	01.13.00
on litle carpet 2 yards of liniswoolsie	00.13.00
3 remnants of cotton 4 yards and od measure	00.10.00
2 yards of linsiwolsie that is mild	00.08.00
8 porrigers 3 cadl pots 1 pint drinking pot and a drinking cup with a flagon	01.05.06
1 chest 28 yards of new cloath 2s per yard	02.03.00
1 cass and bottels with 1 pair of Irish stockings	00.07.00
2 chairs 2 cuishons 2 yards 1.2 cours [coarse] linen	00.07.00
4 yards of cotton and linen	00.08.00
1 tabl cloath	00.10.00
4 yard 3/4 canves	00.07.06
4 yards 3.4 mor of canvis	00.07.06
2 ould blanckets 1 ould packing cloath	00.06.00
2 remnants of stuff	00.02.00
3 pillow beers 5 napkins 3 towells	00.10.00
2 sives 1 basket 2 bodkins	00.04.02
2 pounds of yarne woolin and linin	00.05.00
1 clos stoole and 1 litl glass cas	00.06.00
1 fether bed 1 pillow 1 bolster 2 blanckets 1 coverlid with 1 bed steed	03.10.00
2 blanckets deliverd to Henry Bowen	00.10.00
6 sausers 4 small dishes 2 candlsticks 1 chamber pot	00.15.00

1 feather boulster & 3 yards of dimitie	01.00.00
1 chest 2 ould green rugs	01.04.00
6 paine & on od speet	06.00.00
18 napkins & towell 15 pillow beers or towells or napkins	01.12.00
1 trunck 5s 1 trunck more 6s	00.11.00
1 table and forme	00.06.00
1 canopie for the bed	00.15.00
1 chest	00.02.00
apls in 2 chambers	01.00.00
1 steel mill	00.10.00
1 pannell & 3 lins	00.05.00
in wool 49 13d forth	02.13.05
1 woollin wheel & an ould chest	00.07.00
27 pound of flax 13d for	01.09.03
3 ould cart rope & 7 forks	00.15.06
1 bed 1 boolster 1 pillow 2 sheets 1 blancket 1 rugg & coverlit 1 small fether bed with 1 small ould boster & bedsteed	04.00.00
1 costeet 3 piks	02.00.00
1 woolin wheel and hemp in stalks & 2 bed steads with ould matts	00.05.00
22 soft cheeses being 78 pound	01.00.00
2 fowling peeces & on cutles	02.00.00
24 cheeses being 83 pound	01.07.08
57 of pewter & 18 2 sansers	04.05.06
1 ould pewter dish waits & skalls	00.06.04
2 drinking potts waits & skalls & 1 candle stick	00.08.00
1 ould small flagin and 3 drinking potts	00.07.00
2 drinking potts to chamber potts & 1 candle stick	00.08.00
2 poringers 2 candlestick 1 sawser & botl	

1 salt siller 1 drinking up 1 vine cup	
with ould pewter	00.09.00
in tinn warr 6 peeces	00.03.00
1 bras [brass] cettel [kettle] & 4 milk panns of brass	01.10.00
6 bras cettels & 4 scillits [skillets]	04.00.00
1 cettle 2 scillits bell metl & 1 chaffing dish	
1 ladl 2 scimers 3 candlesticks 1 thine	
2 Bras cettls 2 bras cover	00.14.00
2 bras pots on [one] Iron pott	00.15.00
pestl & morter & warming pann	00.14.00
9 peeses of earthen warre 1 lanthern	
& on gratter & on heckell	00.09.00
8 bottoms of yarn & 3 bunches of flax	00.03.00
1 basket & trenchers in it & 2 tapps	00.02.00
2 paire cobirons 1 iron 1 paire of tongs 1	
fire shoovell	00.18.00
1 peel 2 fine forrks 1 fork & 3 spitts	01.00.00
1 small table 3 chairs 4 stools	00.08.00
9 napkins a litl tabl cloath	00.08.00
1 litl napsack & 8 spoons 11 trenchers	00.03.06
2 lamps 2 spoons 1 morter	00.05.06
1 box with the suger in it & pepper	00.06.00
1 drinkin sack 1 shreding knife and clever	00.03.00
3 pails 2 platters & 1 ould paile	00.05.00
lumber in the meale room with 1 cetl	00.06.00
1 chees pres with milk vessells & a bottl	00.15.00
1 ould sadl 1 tab 1 new barll 1 little	
tabl & small lumber	00.17.00
1 ould pott of Iron with 1 hole in it	00.05.00
cleans beatl rings & wedges 3 axes	01.00.00
in the seller tubs and other caske	01.00.00
1 yoak shackl and pinn	00.05.00

Item	Value
3 trammells 1 crosscut saw 2 windbls	00.13.00
ould Iron 2 tramells 1 gridiron pott hooks 1 hammer 3 litl hooks	00.15.00
5 cows & 2 oxen	30.00.00
dung and grindston	00.15.00
8 planck 300 boards	01.00.00
300 clove boards & polls	00.10.00
1 cart & wheels	04.00.00
1 plow 1 ould plow	00.11.00
12 ewe sheepe	07.04.00
3 weathers 1 ram	01.12.00
2 ew lambs	00.16.00
Indian corn About 70 bushells	07.00.00
haie in the barne	12.00.00
oats 15s 4 swine	05.00.00
1 hors 1 cow	13.15.00
16 cerkes	01.04.00
pott hooks shovell 3 forks 1 raak 1 yoake 1 hack	00.12.00
in mony 23 in peag	28.10.10
molt 10 bushells	02.12.00
in wheat 2 bushells	00.12.00
26 bushells of indian corn	02.12.00
ould Iron beetle rings chaine and padlock	00.06.00
buter about 19 L [pounds]	00.08.00
20 ackers of medow	80.00.00
the hows and land About it	190.00.00
1 lott ner stonie river let to John Pierpoint for years	40.00.00
in the great lotts 1 pastur of About 2o Accers	40.00.00
About 10 Accers of land ner the great lotts & 12 Accers bought of Thomas Garner	[not legible]
1 peer [pair] of new cloath at bro [Brother] Pierpoints	03.10.00

185

1 box in the parler	00.03.60
1 brass pott	00.05.00
1 ould warming pann	00.01.00
1 pillyon	00.07.00
2 more smothing Irons	00.02.00
2 bushells of barly by Isaack Johnson	00.08.00
in peagg 1 bushell 1/2 indian corn by Mr. Robert Pepper	00.09.00
in wood prised at	00.15.00
2 paire linm 4 ould haows	00.02.00
Appls in the two orchyards yet to gather	00.04.00
2 linin wheels	00.03.00
1 new halter for A hors 1 bucket with what belongs to the well	00.04.00
in fowls	00.15.00
in total	623.01.06
debts by spesiallties	38.00.00
1 coult	05.00.00
mor in dets	01.05.00
mor in debts	01.13.08
6 boxes	00.12.00
in Jarcie yarne	00.04.00
Total approximately:	668.00.00

At A meeting of ye magistr 15 October 1659 Capt Isack Johnson, Robert Pepper deposed saith that this is a trew Inventory of the estate of the late John Johnson to ye best of theire knowledge.

Readers are encouraged to return to the beginning of John Johnson's inventory to read it room by room. By doing so, readers will get a glimpse of the type of furnishings in each room. It is clear that Isaac Johnson and Robert Pepper inventoried each room in the smallest detail in John Johnson's house, the barn and outbuildings, as well as assessed his land holdings and animals.

An estate valued at over 600 Pounds in the Seventeenth Century would have been considered extraordinarily high for the times. This valuation seems consistent with the view of visitors to Roxbury in the middle 17th Century that the people were wealthy. John Johnson's inventory reveals that he had no less than six beds and sufficient bedding in his house as well as rugs and carpets in each of the rooms. Furthermore, he had scores and scores of napkins that might reveal in addition for a penchant for cleanliness, but also a person of dignity and class. The number of books he had [eight] plus a Bible and a Psalm Book is small in number but helps us understand that John Johnson could read.

> *[Note: It is not clear what happened to the 90 books that Richard Mather borrowed from John Johnson and William Park.]*

Inasmuch as his original house burned to the ground in 1645, it is possible to assume that his estate inventory *[except for certain apparel and "trifles" saved from the house fire]* was made up of purchases and acquisitions between 1645 and 1659.

CHAPTER SIXTEEN

THE LEGACIES OF JOHN JOHNSON'S PURITAN SOCIETY

There have been many debates whether or not the Puritan Society of New England in the 1600's had any influences on, or supplied any legacies for, the American Society of the Twenty-first Century. Depending upon one's understanding in regard to how the motivation for emigration shapes one's views, we can believe the Puritans left us with legacies nonetheless. It still leaves room to believe that other forms of government or events could have shaped the American Society.

It is clear that John Johnson was mostly motivated by the possibility to worship as a Puritan, free of the Church of England. While emigrants who came later in the Seventeenth Century to America might have had a more secular rather than sacred motivation, John Johnson typified the "perfect Puritan."

Regardless of one's leanings about the motivation for emigration, the Puritan Society did make several contributions to the generations that followed. Aspects of the Puritan legacies have both positive and negative implications. These contributions are: organization of government; democracy; conduct of the citizenry; education; work; law; Church; moral conscience; personal freedom; political freedom; commerce; social freedom; attitudes about minorities, servants and infant damnation; national pride; and, even fascination with death.

The issue of the organization of governance in America is based upon the concepts of the Puritans. Many of these concepts were from their English heritage and experiences. The establishment of towns, counties, colonies [and later, States] provided the beginnings for local control. Even though the relationship between Church and government eventually separated by the Eighteenth Century, local government remained. Democracy in Church [Meeting Houses] rule led to democracy in town meetings and one's desire for the ability to influence decisions that affected them.

A court system of Magistrates and Deputies gave way to the Supreme Court and the Federal and State courts systems of today.

In the Puritan Society, the community at large was responsible for the conduct of all of the citizens whether or not they were Puritans. Now we rely upon rules, regulations, and laws to govern conduct. These rules, regulations, and laws vary little from State to State.

The Puritans wasted no time in the establishment of "free schools." While these schools did not begin as school for every citizen [reserved for Puritans only], the importance of education was eventually made available to everyone because the "rate" or tax was levied against all citizens.

> *[Note: It is the belief of the author that democracy and fairness prevailed in nearly all Puritan actions in the long run. Many times the outcomes were a result of the Puritan intolerance.]*

Probably the most frequently cited Puritan legacy is that of the "Puritan work ethic." Hard work and long hours as well as thrift were demanded of all citizens, young and old. Everyone had tasks and duties assigned to them regardless of age. No thought was given to child labor laws [there weren't any] or old age retirement [there was not any retirement possible.] These indiscretions against the young and the old has given way to laws regulating age and type of work permitted for those under fifteen or sixteen, and the social system was implemented that made retirement possible. Yet, the attitude about excellence in work and long hours prevails. The motivation now, however, is personal rather than for the good of the Meeting House, town, Colony or the Commonwealth.

In the beginning of the Massachusetts Bay Colony, the first laws were the laws of God as perceived by the Puritans. The Puritans understood the laws of God covered all human action. [1]

"All the sins and good things found in the whole Bible are to be ranked within the compass of the ten Commandments," according to Rev. John Cotton [2]

The early Puritan settlements were fraught with superiority versus inferiority, old over young, husbands over wives. Anne Hutchinson, banished from the Massachusetts Bay Colony, was convicted because she tried to "play the part of a Husband than a Wife, and a preacher than a Hearer, and a Magistrate than a Subject." [3]

Gradually, there was recognition of the sinful nature of man that could not be addressed by the Puritan Society effectively.

The establishment of the government and the court was ultimately the solution to resolve the issue of crime and punishment. Of course, because of the blending of the religion and civil aspects of the Colony, most of the laws that were established were about sins against God and His word.

The influences of the English as well as the laws of the Colonial Period are many in regard to current laws in force in America. American laws, after all, are based upon the Common Laws of England. These Common Laws were precisely the laws brought to the Massachusetts Bay Colony by the Puritans. Wills, probates, land transactions, law suits against others, use of power of attorney, settlement of civil disputes, divorce, and even "sins of the heart" are some of the issues now addressed by American laws with roots in Puritan America.

Democracy in Church and the Puritan rejection of all "things Catholic" in the Church of England probably fostered the growth of many Protestant denominations. Remarkably similar in many ways to the Puritan leanings are the fundamental Churches that are so prevalent in almost every community in Twenty-first Century

America. Church government in some denominations demonstrates the Puritan system of self-rule and a "congregational way," as it is called.

There is almost a paradox in regard to the legacy of a moral conscience left us by the Puritan. They were not, of course, immune from various "sins or moral infidelities." The family system inherited from the English clearly prevailed in the Massachusetts Bay Colony. The one main difference, however, was that in the Puritan Society, the leaders enforced the "moral code" including those of a sexual nature. Our dual system of recognizing marriage [civil and religious] may be a result of the Puritans making marriage a civil contract rather than a Church event. [4]

A good example of Puritan moral values included the attitude and the laws regarding sex. The Puritans viewed sexual activity between men and women outside of a marriage as sinful. But the penalty might be a fine and a public punishment at the Meeting House. On the other hand, there was a general acknowledgment that some sexual sins such as sexual violence, bestiality, buggery, and pedophilia deserved punishment by death.

Roughly, in about twenty-five per cent of the marriages in New England, the brides were pregnant. The Puritans thought than the eventual marriage would lessen the sin of pre-marital sex. Regardless, each year of the Colonial Period showed a rise in bastard births.

Many laws of the Colonial Period have been removed from the books. Adultery, once a reason for punishment by death, is merely a civil law issue now.

The connection between the laws of the Colonial Period and the Bible are well-established by the selected examples listed below. [5]

> *[Note: Current Laws in the American Society*
> *continue to carry a significant influence from the*
> *Bible whether from the Jewish Torah or the*

SAMPLES OF PURITAN LAWS AND BIBLE JUSTIFICATIONS

Law and Bible References

Forcing of a maide, or a rape, is not
to be punished with death by God's laws,
with fine, or penalty to the father of the
maid. With marriage of the maid defiled,
Deut. 22.17, 18 & 28, 29

to wit, if she and her father consent
With corporall punishment of stripes, for
this wrong is a real slander, and it is
worse to make a whore, than to say one is
a whore.

Fornication to be purnished
By marriage of the maid, or giving her
Exo. 22, 16

a sufficient dowry.
With stripes, though fewer, from the equity
of the former case.

Maiming or wounding of a freeman,
Ex. 21. 18, 19

whether free burgesse or free inhabitant,
to be punished with a fine, and to pay
Lev. 24.19, 20

Rebellious children, whether they

Deut. 21, 18-20

continue in riott or drunkenness, after
Ex. 21. 15, 17

due correction from their parents, or
Lev. 20. 9

whether they curse or smite their parents,
to be put to death.

Murder, which is a willfull manslaughter,
Ex. 21.12,13

not in a mans necessary defence, nor
Num. 35. 16,17 18

casually committed, but out of hatred or
21-28. 30 to 33.

cruelty, to be punished with death.
Gene. 9. 6

Adultery, which is the defyling of the
marriage bed to be punished with death.
Deut. 22. 22 and Lev. 20.10

Incest, which is the defiling of any that are
neare of kinne within the degrees prohibited
in Leviticus, to be punished with death;
unnatural filthiness to be punished with
death; whether sodomy, which is carnal
fellowship of man with man, or of woman with
woman, or buggery, which is carnall fellowship
of man or soman with beasts or fowles.
Lev. 20.11,12,13,14, & 19, 20, 21.

Pollution of a woman knowne to be

in her flowers, to be punished with death.
Lev. 20.18

Whoredome of a maid in her fathers house
Deut. 22. 20, 21

kept secret till after her marriage with another,
to be punished with death.

Manstealing to be punished with death.
Deut. 24, 7

False witness against life to be punished with death.
Deut. 19. 16, 21.

The Puritans of 1630, locked into Puritan dogma from their parents and others, thought that the physical nature of sex was "polluting and vile." [6] Therefore, since there was no distinction between Church and State, sin was addressed by legal penalty.

The first line of control of the morality of the citizens in New England was always the household. Young people were always under the government of the family. Single adults were not allowed to live alone but were required to live with a Puritan family. Society continues to struggle with moral conscience issues.

Puritan laws, as had been hoped, did not promote moral conscience, and 21st Century laws have not lessened immoral acts.

Perhaps because of the rigid and overpowering control the Puritans exerted over Puritans and non-Puritans alike, a great desire for personal freedom developed. Of course, an emerging democracy would naturally lead to recognition of the rights of the individual as well as free will of its citizens. It is ironic that the Puritans could not foresee the direction the country was going because of, and in spite of, its attitudes and laws.

"Ask not what the country can do for you, but what you can do for the country" as intoned by President John F. Kennedy, might have been said just as well in the Seventeenth Century Massachusetts Bay Colony. Scholars of the Colonial Period of American History have debated, but have not under-estimated, the dedication the Early Puritans had toward its Society and its "Manifest Destiny." The Puritans truly believed that the Massachusetts Bay Colony was the beginning of a new Israel---straight out of the Old Testament of the Bible. National pride gradually developed with every skirmish with the Native Americans, with every political and legal win over England, and ultimately with the results of the Revolutionary War. National confidence had been firmly established by 1776.

Interesting negative aspects of the Puritan Society has resulted in positive [yet, late in coming] attitudes about minorities, servants, status, and infant damnation.

First of all, the Puritans believed that the Native Americans and later the African-Americans, were inferior "just like the Canaanites" all of whom were in need of salvation. It was the position of the Puritans that it was their duty to convert these pagan people.

Further, white and black servants in the Colonial Period of America were treated indifferently in addition to being forever indentured to someone of a higher class. John Johnson, himself, had a servant "ordered to him by the General Court" who served John Johnson for a period of three years with minimal pay. Apparently, this servant had been mistreated by a fellow Puritan resulting in the placement with Captain Johnson.

In the Massachusetts Bay Colony there was a status carryover from England that had to do with education, type of profession, wealth or inherited English title or any combination of these factors. This social structure continues to exist to a certain extent. The difference between the year 1630 and the year 2000 is the existence of a huge middle class. John Johnson, if his land holdings, value of his Estate, and civic responsibilities are indicative, was not in the lower strata of the Colony.

In this world there will always be differences between people: color, education, profession, wealth. But it does seem like less and less importance is given to what is different between Americans.

Perhaps the message from John Johnson, who had education, wealth, and civic importance but no social distinction, that it was not necessary to be higher in human status than his peers to enjoy the fruits of his labor. After all, readers are reminded that the goal of every Puritan was Heaven.

The Puritans had a real fascination about death. This interest was due likely to their religious beliefs about salvation and Heaven. Mournful physical displays of emotions were the norm in the 17th Century but so were written forms of mournfulness expressed. Some cultures and surely some faiths are more accepting and matter-of-fact about death.

It is interesting to note that the Puritan spent literally all of his or her time and energy for the coming of death [and Heaven] and to have those left behind express themselves so morbidly is unusual. There are parallels in our American society that are perhaps a carryover from the Puritan times.

Rooted in the democracy of the Puritan Meeting House is the ability in our American society to have differing political views as well as the ability to express them. Puritans had the freedom to discuss, and even vote, on issues at the Meeting House that affected them. It is true that only freemen [citizens] who were Puritans could vote. However, this requirement of Puritan-only citizenship was eliminated by 1664. First Amendment rights guaranteed in the American Constitution must have been a result of the growing democracy in the Puritan community.

Robert Keayne, a Colony merchant, was fined by the General Court for over-charging customers for nails in the early 1630's. Obviously things got a lot better for the merchants after that. The Puritan Society, as a communal adventure, eventually developed a strong commerce with other colonies and with England. The problems of taxes, free trade, and merchant income of the period between 1630-1700, progressively led to legislation that has affected current laws and regulations regarding business practices here and abroad.

Infant damnation during the Colonial Period had to do with children who were born with birthmarks and other signs of abnormality. The Puritans believed that such marks and abnormalities were signs of the devil. Their attitude about witches, of course, is well-known. Generally speaking, the current American society does not believe that children born with abnormalities are the work of the devil.

The emerging social freedom by 1700 was a direct result of the eventual acceptance by the Puritans of others with differing views. One must remember that the Puritans were essentially becoming outnumbered with each emigration and with each successive generation. Furthermore, there was an individual desire to move west and south for more opportunities of income-producing farm land. The continued migration of non-Puritans from 1640 to after the English Civil Wars helped nudge the issue of freedom of choice to the forefront.

The writers of the Constitution appropriately debated and chose the laws of governance based upon the positives as well as the negatives of the previous 150 years of Colonial rule.

Our Constitution has been changed little but modeled frequently and freely by other countries in their quest for democracy and freedom. While much credit should be given to the Constitutional Conventions and the work of those who signed the Constitution, the 1630 Puritans of the Massachusetts Bay Colony set the initial ground work for the country as we have come to know it.

In A Literary History of the American People, Volume One, author Charles Angoff, said of the Puritans, "it is no exaggeration to say that nearly all that was written in the Colonies in the Seventeenth Century, in both prose and verse, was rubbish, and that as far as its literacy merit is concerned it deserves to be forgotten." [7] Angoff does cite three writers who deserve recognition: Rev. John Eliot for his kindly character and genuinely Christian attitude toward the Indians; Thomas Morton because he was one of the most intelligent men of his generation yet was denounced as a disturber of the peace and a nuisance; and, the Reverend Roger Williams because he was the first apostle of liberty of conscience in the land [and was the first preacher to be banished from the Massachusetts Bay Colony for his liberal principles.]

Angoff continues "the early New Englanders were so wrought up with their religion that their minds were constantly filled with gloom and the most horrible foreboding. They believed in signs, devils and bad omens. [8] Puritans were overly concerned about morals and the issuing of stiff discipline for offenders. Even the General Court "forbade short sleeves "whereby the nakedness of the arms may be discovered" and forbade long hair among men.[9] Amusement of any kind was not to be enjoyed and no one was to engage in "domestic affections" on a Sunday.

> [Note: Puritans believed that a child born on a Sunday meant that the parents must have conceived the child on a Sunday.]

While Charles Angoff had nothing positive to say about the Puritans and the Colonial Period, particularly the literature, the Puritans, despite the lack of citations of positive contributions by some historians, deserve our acknowledgment. Somehow Angoff did not understand that the arts are a reflection of the times and the people rather than vice versa. Clearly, all sermons, stories, poems, verse, prose, newspapers, legal briefs, letters, and annals were a product of people who were entrenched in the Puritan way of life.

Perhaps the strongest and most important legacy of the Puritan period upon the American society was how the practices and problems of the Puritans influenced the thinking and planning of the United States Constitution. The issue of separation of Church and State is likely a result of the recognition that a religion, such as that practiced by the Puritans, was not effective in providing a true democracy for all of the people of the country. Article V of the United States Constitution provides that...."the Senators and Representatives before mentioned, and the Members of the several State Legislatures, and all executive and judicial Officers, both of the United States and of the several States, shall be bound by Oath or Affirmation, to support this Constitution; **but no religious test shall ever be required as a Qualification to any Office or public Trust under the United States."** [10]

Further, the very first Amendment ratified in 1791 of first ten Amendments (called the Bill of Rights) to the United States Constitution provides that...."**Congress shall make no law respecting an establishment of religion,** or prohibiting the free exercise thereof; or abridging the freedom of speech, or of the press, or the right of the people peaceably to assemble, and to petition the Government for a redress of grievances." [11]

It is clear from the United States Constitution and its First Amendment that the fathers of America had the understanding of the society's problems that were a result of the Puritan beliefs and practices.

Without the desire for a life less dull and dreary, the increase of a rich middle class, and the desire for personal pursuit of happiness, the negatives of the Puritan society were transformed into positives. We should not underestimate the contributions of the Puritans regardless of the reasons why the changes in our society came to be.

CHAPTER SEVENTEEN

SOME CONCLUSIONS ABOUT
JOHN JOHNSON

Now that the life of John Johnson has been explored, what can be said about John Johnson, the man? Thousands and thousands of genealogy books, biographical sketches, and books of remembrance have resulted in "writings of vanity" about ancestors the various writers. It was not the intent of this book to do that. For example, would it not be interesting to know why the residents of Roxbury believed that John Johnson was not "meeting their expectations?" Does the reader wonder why John Johnson might have used "red oak" in a house he was building for Joshua Foote in Boston when he was requested to use only white or black oak? The goal was to reflect on all aspects of John Johnson.

But in spite of the infrequent references to problems John Johnson had in New England, it becomes clear that a portrait of the man is possible to determine. As Captain Edward Johnson of Woburn said, "to write the history of John Johnson would fill a volume, and his worth as one of the founders of the government of the colonies of Massachusetts is too well-known to be recorded here." [in the History of Essex County, Massachusetts with Biographical Sketches, Vol. II].

First of all, John Johnson was an educated man. He could read and write. John Johnson was interested in having a school available for his own children as well as the other residents of Roxbury. He donated property for the first school and financially supported its operation.

John Johnson was a man who gave all of his life for the benefit of the Massachusetts Bay Colony and town of Roxbury. He was known as a man of great civic responsibility and civic affairs.

Furthermore, he was selected to represent the Massachusetts Bay Colony in dealing with the other New England colonies as well as being elected as a "Selectman" or representative to the embryo government of the Colony. John Johnson was constable for Roxbury for many, many years. Practically from the beginning, he was "Surveyor-General of the Arms" for the Massachusetts Bay Colony until his death in 1659. He was trusted with the storing of the gun powder and arms used in the defense of the Colony. John Johnson served as a juror of his peers at the General Court.

He was trusted by his fellow residents to provide inventory of their assets upon their death. Likewise, the Magistrates appointed him to provide an inventory of assets of those outside of Roxbury, Massachusetts on numerous occasions.

Because of his knowledge of surveying and engineering that he might have learned in England or had experience doing there, John Johnson was appointed many times to "lay the boundaries between various towns in Massachusetts. He was asked to build various highways, fences, cart paths and bridges in Roxbury. He helped connect Boston with outlying towns with bridges and highways.

John Johnson was involved with the military effort in the Massachusetts Bay Colony from 1630 to 1659. Not only was he the Captain of the Roxbury Military Company, he was the clerk [not the Captain of, as one genealogy reported] of the Ancient and Honorable Artillery Company of Massachusetts. In England, John Johnson likely was a member of the Honourable Artillery Company of London that was a model for the Massachusetts Company.

John Johnson was a religious man. He was a staunch Puritan. It is interesting that though the Puritans and the Pilgrims long rejected the Book of Common Prayer used in The Church of England, John Johnson had a copy of the Book of Common Prayer in the inventory of his assets upon his death. John Johnson was one of the original founders of the First Church of Roxbury, and was involved with the calling of Rev. John Eliot, a fellow Puritan, to be its preacher. Johnson was likely involved in the construction of the First Church of Roxbury, and was appointed to make repairs on the structure on at least one occasion.

The word of John Johnson was sought out and trusted on behalf of inquiries made by the Magistrates about legal issues of Massachusetts Bay Colony residents.

John Johnson was a family man who cared for and provided for his children, and loved his wife, Grace. His home, based upon his inventory, was large and comfortable. He was a leader of his family by example, and most likely worked hard because he did accumulate a large estate that provided those things necessary for comfort.

He was a businessman. John Johnson had a farm that provided wheat, barley, and corn for sale to the Colony. He was involved with animal husbandry that produced calves and goats he sold to others. Johnson owned a tavern in Roxbury. His ability to compute helped him in his responsibilities as the keeper of the ammunition. John Johnson was a landowner and land dealer. Not only did John Johnson provide land for his sons, Isaac Johnson and Humphrey Johnson, that was customary in Colonial New England. He bought and sold property for a profit, also.

John Johnson possessed the elements of character that even today's society values tries to instill. That is, Johnson had great integrity. Even though the Puritan Society fell apart because of conservative views and other rigid practices, John Johnson did not deviate on his path to Heaven. He must have been very well-organized and focused. He could not have provided for his family from his farm, build bridges, decide boundaries, testify in Court, represent people as attorney and power of attorney, keep the Colony's powder and arms, as well as represent Roxbury at the General Court as a Selectman, without the benefit of organization and focus.

John Johnson had a high sense of responsibility to others as well as his community. The writer does not believe that Johnson did all these things for his own glory or honor. Remember this is a man who was, by all accounts, a commoner without the title of "Sir," and without having been called "Mister," except for three or four written references. Instead, he was respectfully called either "Captain" or "Goodman" Johnson both terms that were probably more to his own liking.

Courage is a character trait that is evident in his sense of adventure. He left England as an adventurer, a man who conquered the unknown. John Johnson was a man who calculated the risks to his family and to himself, but who had the self-confidence and courage to persevere in his "errand in the wilderness."

His selection as overseer of wills of his friends and his selection to take inventory of the estates reveals that he was an honest and trustworthy man.

John Johnson, in his small way, contributed to the eventual development of the democratic society we call *America*. We will never know for certain whether John Johnson was a visionary. But he did what he had to do and what he was asked to do at the time.

By all accounts John Johnson was *"An Uncommon Man in the Commonwealth of the Massachusetts Bay Colony from 1630 to 1659."*

NOTES

Chapter One   The Puritans and Their Society

1. Compton's Encyclopedia Online v.2.0. The Learning Company, 1997.

2. Compton's, 3.

3. Micah 4: 1,2 ; Ezekiel 17: 22. King James Bible (Nashville: Thomas Nelson, 1976).

4. Reese, M.M. The Puritan Impulse: The English Revolution, 1559-1660 (London: A. & C. Black, 1975) 246.

5. Smith, J.R. Pilgrims and Adventurers (Chelmsford: Essex Record Office, 1992). 28-29.

6. Geree, John. The Character of an Old English Puritan or Non-Conformist (London: W. Wilson, 1636.). 38-9.

7. Reuben, Paul P. "Chapter: Puritanism and Colonial Period to 1770" PAL: Perspectives in American Literature - A Research and Reference Guide. www.url: http://www.csustan.edu/english/reuben/pal/chap1.html November 12, 1998.

8. Feldmeth, Greg D. "U.S. History" Resources: http://home.earthlink.net/~gfeldmeth/ USHistory.html March 31, 1998.

9. Oliver, Peter. The Puritan Commonwealth (Boston: Little, Brown, 1856). 193.

10. Prince, Thomas. Chronological History of New England (Boston: Cummings, Hilliard, 1826). 322.

11. Prince, 394.

12. Prince, 394.

13. Prince, 413.

14. Price, Martin. <u>The Restoration and the Eighteenth Century</u> (New York: Oxford UP, 1973).

15. Prince, 275

16. Prince, 275

17. Prince, 216.

18. Hansen, Marcus L. <u>The Atlantic Migration</u>, 1607-1860 (New York: Harper & Row, 1940) 32.

19. Hansen, 32.

20. Benton, Josiah H. <u>Warning Out in New England</u> (Freeport: Books for Libraries Press, 1970) 8.

21. Benton, 46-51.

22. Benton, 19.

23. Benton, 38.

24. Benton, 43.

25. Boston <u>Sermons</u>. 1671-1679, Manuscript (Boston Massachusetts Historical Society, 1972.

26. Morgan, Edmund S. <u>The Puritan Family</u> (New York: Harper & Row, 1966) 47.

27. Morgan, 48.

28. Morgan, 52.

29. Hawke, David F. Everyday Life in Early America (New York: Harper & Row, 1988) 93.

30. Hawke, 93.

31. Pomfret, John E. Founding the American Colonies 1583-1660 (New York: Harper & Row, 1817) 173.

32. Pomfret, 174.

33. Hawkes, 109-10.

34. Reuben, VII.

35. Reuben, VIII.

36. Miller, Perry. Errand Into the Wilderness (Cambridge: Belnap Press of HUP, 1956).

Chapter Two   **Adventurers and The Formation of Companies in Establishing New England**

1. Gardner, Lucie M. The Settlers About Boston Bay Prior to 1630 (Salem: Salem Press, 1910) 3.

2. Gardner, 3.

3. Gardner, 4.

4. Gardner, 5.

5. Leder, Lawrence H. America 1603 - 1789 (Minneapolis: Burgess Publishing Company, 1972) 41.

6. Leder, 53.

7. Leder, 54.

8. Anderson, Robert Charles. "Congregations in Flight" <u>The American Genealogist</u>. July/October, 1997). 257-261.

9. Tyack, Norman C.P. <u>Migration to New England from East Anglia</u> (London: ULP, 1951) 8.

10. Tyack, 15.

11. Thompson, Roger. <u>Mobility and Migration</u> (Amherst: UMP, 1994) 186.

12. Thompson, 189.

13. New England Historic Genealogical Society. <u>NEHGS Register</u> Volume 8, "The Johnson Family" (Boston: NEHGS, 1854) 358.

14. Thompson, 203.

Chapter Three   **John Johnson's Motivation to Migrate to America**

1. Thompson, Roger F. "Continuing my research." E-mail to Gerald Johnson. March 2, 1999.

2. Tyack, Norman P.C. <u>Migration from East Anglia to New England before 1660</u>, Ph.D. diss., University of London, 1951, 102.

3. Anderson, Virginia D. <u>New England's Generation</u> (Cambridge: CUP, 1991) 16.

4. Tyack, 102.

5. Tyack, 103-4.

6. Anderson, 33-4.

7. Anderson, 196.

8. Force, Peter, ed., <u>Tracts and Other Papers Relating Principally to the Origin, Settlement, and Progress of the Colonies in North America</u> (Washington, D.C., 1838) II.

9. Anderson, 196.
10. Thompson, Roger F. <u>Mobility and Migration</u> (Amherst: UMP, 1994) 7-13.

Chapter Four   **The Winthrop Fleet**

1. Banks, Charles E. <u>The Winthrop Fleet</u> (Baltimore: Genealogical Publishing Company, 1983) 18.

2. Rose-Troup, Frances. <u>The Massachusetts Bay Colony</u> (New York: Grafton Publishing Company, 1930).

3. Winthrop, Robert C. <u>Life and Letters of John Winthrop, Vol. I</u> (Boston: Little, Brown, 1869) 296.

4. Winthrop, I, 214, 301.

5. Thompson, Roger. <u>Mobility and Migration</u> (Amherst: The University of Massachusetts Press, 1994) 227.

6. Banks, Charles E. <u>The Winthrop Fleet</u> (Baltimore: Genealogical Publishing Company, 1983) 34.

7. Young, Alexander. <u>Chronicles of the first planters of the colony of Massachusetts Bay, 1623-1636</u> (Boston: C.C. Little and J. Brown, 1846) 266.

8. Young, 267.

9. Banks, 58-99.

Chapter Six   **The Marriages of John Johnson**

1. Richardson, Douglas. "The Heath Connection" <u>New England Historic and Genealogical Society</u> (Boston: NEHGS, July, 1992) 262.

2. Richardson, 270.
3. Winters, W<u>. Memorials of the Pilgrim Fathers</u> (Waltham Abbey: Churchyard, 1882) 241.

4. Smith, Dean C., ed. Melinde Lutz Sandborn, <u>The Ancestry of Emily Jane Angell</u> (Boston: NEHGS, 1992). 377-9.

5. Thwing, Walter Eliot. <u>History of the First Church in Roxbury</u> (Boston: Butterfield, 1908) 45.

6. Torrey, Clarence A.<u>Early Marriages in New England Prior to 1700</u> (Baltimore: Genealogical Publishing Company, 1987).

7. Smith, Dean C., ed. Melinde Lutz Sanborn, <u>The Ancestry of Emily Jane Angell</u> (Boston: NEHGS, 1992). 377.

8. Bitler, Janet J. and David B. Scudder. <u>Scudder Searches</u> (Arlington: Scudder Association, 1992) 4.

9. Johnson, Paul Franklin. <u>The Genealogy of Captain John Johnson of Roxbury, Mass</u> (Los Angeles: The Commonwealth Press, 1951) 1.

10. Jacobus, D.K. and W. H. Wood. "Scudders" American Antiquarian Society, Vol. VII, (Worcester: AAS, 1943) and, Skudder, Simon, editor "The Will of William Scudder of

Darenth, 1607" <u>Scudder Wills and Willa Scuddinga</u> (Bristol: The Scudder Association, 1995).

11. Bitler, Janet J., 4.

12. Dorrington, J.B. "Records" <u>Scudder Family Records</u> (London: International Research Publication, 1972) 14.

Chapter Seven   **The Churches of John Johnson**

1. Ware, Hertfordshire (FHL Microfilm 991,326) Hertford Record Office, Hertford, England and Great Amwell, Hertfordshire (FHL Microfilm 991,303) Hertford Record Office, Hertford, England.

2. Hunt, Edith M. <u>The History of Ware</u> (Hertford: Stephen Austin and Sons, Ltd., 1986) 84-5.

3   Ware, Hertfordshire (FHL Microfilm 991,326) Hertford Record Office, Hertford, England and Great Amwell, Hertfordshire (FHL Microfilm 991,202, Hertford Record Office, Hertford, England.

4. Hunt, 86.

5.   Doree, Stephen G., editor, <u>The Parish Register and Tithing Book of Thomas Hassall</u> of Amwell (Cambridge: E. & E. Plumridge Ltd., 1989, 35-40.

6. Doree, vi.

7. Thwing, Walter E. <u>History of the First Church in Roxbury</u> (Boston: W. A. Butterfield, 1908) 25-7.

8. Tercentenary Committee, <u>Tercentenary Celebration of the First Church in Roxbury</u> (Roxbury: Tercentenary Committee, MCMXXX, 1930) 17.

9. Tercentenary Committee, 20.

10. Tercentenary Committee, 19.

11. Prince, Thomas. <u>Annals of New England, Vol. II</u> (Boston: B. Edes and J. Gill, 1755) 64.

12. Thwing, 28.

Chapter Eight   The Ancestry of John Johnson

1. NEGHS <u>Register</u>, Vol. 8, article, "The Johnson Family" (Boston: NEHGS, 1854).

2. Anderson, Robert C. The <u>Great Migration Begins</u> (Boston: NEHGS, 1995) 1104-5.

3. Landon, Emily C. <u>Pepper Genealogy</u> (Bath, (NY) Press of the Steuben Advocate, 1932) 12-14.

4. Private letter, Lynda Hotchkiss, Lincolnshire, England genealogist to Gerald G. Johnson dated November 27, 1998.

5. Private letter, Lynda Hotchkiss, Lincolnshire, England genealogist to Gerald G. Johnson dated November 27, 1998.

1. Annual Report of the Cemetery Department of the City of
    Boston for the Fiscal Year 1902-1903, (Boston: Municipal
    Printing Office, 1903). 1, 40-41.

2. Richardson, Douglas. "The Heath Connection." 1992 The New
    England Historical and Genealogical Register,Vol. CXLVI
    (Boston: New England Historic and Genealogical Society,
    1992). 261-277.

3. Smith, Dean C., Sandborn, Melinde L., editor. The Ancestry of
    Emily Jane Angell. (Boston: New England Historic
    Genealogical Society, 1992)   377-390.

4. Anderson, Robert C. The Great Migration Begins. Vol. II
    (Boston: New England Historical and Genealogical Society,
    1995) 1104-1110.

5. Landon, Emily C. The Pepper Genealogy (Angola: n.p., 1932)
    9-11.

6. Ware, Hertfordshire. Family History Library (LDS) microfilms
    991, 303 and 991, 326. 1998.

7. Doree, Stephen G., editor. The Parish Register and Tithing
    Book of Thomas Hassall of Amwell. Hertfordshire Record
    Society Publication, 4 (Cambridge: Cambridge UP, 1989). 1-
    224.

8. Ullman, Helen S. "William Bartram of Lynn and Swansea,
    Mass: How many wives?" The Essex Genealogist, Vol. VI,
    Number 4 (Lynnfield: Essex Society of Genealogists, 1986)
    178-185.

9. Lawson, Stephen M. J. Johnson Family.
    http://sml.simplenet.com/smlawson/johnsonj.htm.
    1998.

Chapter Ten　　　　**The Education of John Johnson**
　　　　　　　　　　　　and His Children in England

1. Hurd, D. Hamilton. <u>History of Essex County, Massachusetts</u> Vol. II (Philadelphia: J.W. Lewis, 1888) 1412.

2. Massachusetts Historical Society. <u>Collections.</u> Vol. VIII, "The Mather Papers" Fourth Series (Cambridge: Press of John Wilson and Son, 1888) 76,77.

3. Simon, Joan. <u>Education and Society in Tudor England</u> (Cambridge: University Printing House, 1967) 297.

4. Simon, 303.

5. Simon, 316-317.

6. Page, William. <u>The Victoria History of Hertfordshire</u> Vol. II (London: A. Constable, 1908), 88.

7. Page, 382.

Chapter Eleven　　　　**The Civil Responsibilities of**
　　　　　　　　　　　　John Johnson

1. Hurd, D. Hamilton. <u>History of Essex County, Massachusetts.</u> <u>Volume I</u> (Philadelphia: J.W. Lewis, 1888) 1412.

2. Hurd, 1412.

3. Field, Edward. <u>The Colonial Tavern</u> (Providence: Preston and Rounds, 1897) 58.

4. Breen, T.H. "Moving to the New World" <u>William and Mary</u> <u>Quarterly, Third Series, Vol XXX, No. 2</u> (Williamsburg: Institute of Early American History and Culture, 1992). 68.

1. Raikes, Lt. Colonel G.A. The Ancient Vellum Book (Roll of members 1611-1682) (London: Richard Bentley and Son, 1890) 8.

2. Raikes, p. x.

3. Raikes, preface

4. Walker, G. Gould. Honourable Artillery Company, 1537-1987 (London: Honourable Artillery Company, Armoury House, 1986).

5. Rutman, Dorsett B. Winthrop's Boston *Institute of Early American History and Culture* (Williamsburg: UNCP, 1865).

6. Breen, T.H. Puritans and Adventurers (New York: Oxford University Press, 1980) 34.

7. Breen, 35.

8. Rutman, 42.

9. Hoffman, Sally, Archivist, Honourable Artillery Company. Private letter. London, 1998.

10. Roberts, Oliver A. History of the Military Company of Massachusetts Vol. I, 1637-1738 (Boston: Alfred Mudge and Sons, 1895) 66.

11. Roberts, 151.

12. Crane, Ellery B. "The Early Militia System of Massachusetts" Massachusetts Historical Society Volume 105 (Boston: Massachusetts Historical Society, 1905) 105-108.

13. Winslow, Edward. Winslow Papers (Boston: Massachusetts Historical Society) undated.

14. Breen, 41.

Chapter Fourteen   The Great John Johnson Fire of 1645

1. Hosmer, James K., editor. Winthrop's Journal "History of New England" 1630-1649 (New York: Charles Scribner's Sons, 1908) 220-221.

2. Hosmer, 292.

Chapter Fifteen   The Complete Will of John Johnson

1. Suffolk County Probate Records #218

2. Suffolk County Wills. Abstracts of the Earliest Wills Upon Record in the County of Suffolk, Massachusetts. (Baltimore: Genealogical Publishing Company, 1984) 156.

Chapter Sixteen   The Legacies of John Johnson's Puritan Society

1. Morgan, Edmond S. The Puritan Family (New York: Harper & Row, 1966) 11.

2. Morgan, 11.

3. Adams, Charles F., editor. Antinomianism in the Colony of Massachusetts Bay (Boston: Prince Society, 1894) 329.

216

4. Cooke, Jacob E., editor. Encyclopedia of the North American Colonies, Vol. II (New York: Charles Scribner, 1993) 685.

5. Hutchinson, Thomas. Comp., A Collection of Original Papers relative to the History of the colony of Massachusetts Bay (Boston: Thomas and John Fleet, 1769) 173-174.

6. Cooke, 684.

7. Angoff, Charles. A Literary History of the American People Volume One (New York: Alfred A. Knopf, 1931) 247.

8. Angoff, 58.

9. Angoff, 59.

10. Maier, Pauline. The Declaration of Independence and The Constitution of the United States (New York: Bantam Books, 1998) 75.

11. Maier, 78.

INDEX

General Index

Names

Abraham Johnson, 62, 66, 70
Agnes Cheney, 47
Alice Prior, 66
Alonzo L. Johnson, 105
Anderson, Robert Charles. *See* Robert Charles Anderson
Anderson, Virginia D.. *See* Virginia D. Anderson
Angell, Emily Jane. *See* Emily Jane Angell
Arthur Johnson, 95, 96
Bachelor, Stephen. *See* Stephen Bachelor, Rev.
Banks, Charles E.. *See* Charles E. Banks
Barnabus Fawer, 49, 170, 171
Benjamin Negus, 49
Beryl Crawley, viii, xvii, xix
Boleyn, Anne. *See* Anne Boleyn
Bridgett Harbottle, 65
Browne, Kellam. *See* Kellam Browne
Burt, Hugh. *See* Hugh Burt
Catherine of Aragon, 2
Cesar Augusto Johnston, viii
Charles E. Banks, 36, 61
Charles Fines, 9
Charles I, King. *See* King Charles I
Charles II, King. *See* King Charles II
Charles M. Ellis, 44
Charles Pope, 130
Cheney, Agnes. *See* Agnes Cheney
Cheney, William. *See* William Cheney
Clement VII, Pope. *See* Pope Clement VII
Cobran, William. *See* William Cobron
Cobron, William. *See* William Cobron

Colbran, William. *See* William Colbron
Cora Elizabeth Hahn Smith, 105
Cotton, Rev. John. *See* John Cotton
Crawley, Beryl. *See* Beryl Crawley
D. Hamilton Hurd, vii, 115
David E. Johnson, xxii
Doree, Stephen. *See* Stephen Doree, Dr.
Douglas Richardson, ix, 48
Dudley, Thomas. *See* Thomas Dudley
Edith Hunt, xiv, xv, xvi
Eliot, Rev. John. *See* John Eliot
Elizabeth I, Queen. *See* Queen Elizabeth I
Elizabeth Johnson, 12, 13, 55, 63, 72, 81, 83, 89, 90, 112, 180
Ellis, Charles M.. *See* Charles M. Ellis
Emily Jane Angell, 205
Fawer, Barnabus. *See* Grace Negus Fawer Johnson
Fawer, Grace Negus. *See* Grace Negus Fawer Johnson
Fiennes, Lady Arbella. *See* Lady Arbella Fiennes
Fines (Fiennes), Charles. *See* Charles Fines
Foote, Joshua. *See* Joshua Foote
Geoffrey Johnson, 65, 66
Gerald G. Johnson, xxxi, 210
Gerald Garth Johnson, 1, 2, x, 106
Gorges, Robert. *See* Robert Gorges
Grace Johnson, 13, 72
Grace Negus, 47, 49, 101
Grace Negus Fawer, 47, 49, 101
Hannah Johnson, 54, 104, 105
Hannah Throckmorton, 65
Harbottle, Bridgett. *See* Bridgett Harbottle

Johnson, Robert. *See* Robert Johnson

Johnson, Sarah. *See* Sarah Johnson

Johnson, Susan. *See* Susan Johnson

Johnson, William. See William Johnson

Johnston, Cesar Augusto. *See* Cesar Augusto Johnston

Joseph Johnson, 54, 55, 84, 104. *See* Joseph Johnson

Joshua Foote, 170, 171, 172, 199

Karlene Johnson Messer, viii

Keayne, Robert. *See* Robert Keayne

Kellam Browne, 6

King Charles I, 9, 21, 42

King Charles II, viii

King Henry VIII, 2, 3, 54, 120

King James I, 1, 2, 20, 26

King James VI, 1

Kozacheck, Thomas. *See* Thomas Kozacheck

Lady Arbella Fiennes, 23, 62

Lady Arbella Johnson, 22, 23, 31

Lawson, Stephen M.. *See* Stephen M. Lawson

LeAnne M. Johnson Shaw, viii

Luther, Rev. Martin, 2

Lynda Hotchkiss, 65, 210

Margery _____. *See* Johnson, Margery

Margery _____, 48, 101

Margery Scudder, 49, 50, 51, 52, 63

Martin Luther, 2, 3

Mary Heath, viii, xi, 8, 23, 28, 31, 36, 39, 43, 44, 47, 49, 51, 53, 54, 55, 62, 73, 79, 81, 82, 84, 94, 99, 101, 165

Mary I, Queen. *See* Queen Mary I

Mary Johnson, 16, 53, 62, 84, 112

Mary Johnson Mowry, 16

Mather, Richard. *See* Richard Mather

Maurice Johnson, 23, 65, 72

McCauley, John. *See* John McCauley

Mehitable Johnson, 13

Melinde Lutz Sanborn, 48, 49, 105, 106, 208

Messer, Karlene Johnson. *See* Karlene Johnson Messer

Miles Standish, 19

Miriam Johnson, ix

Mowry, Mary Johnson. See Mowry, Mary Johsnon. *See* Mary Johnson

Nancy Ticknor Johnson, viii

Negus, Benjamin. *See* Grace Negus Fawer Johnson

Negus, Grace. *See* Grace Negus Fawer Johnson

Nicholas West, 5

Nickole Anne Messer Quackenbush, ix

Norman C.P. Tyack, 26

Nowell, Increase. *See* Increase Nowell

Parks, William. *See* William Parks

Paul Franklin Johnson, 50, 79, 105, 123

Pepper, Robert. *See* Robert Peper

Pinchon, William. *See* William Pinchon

Pope Clement VII, 2, 54

Pope, Charles, 130

Prince, Thomas. *See* Thomas Prince

Prior, Alice. See Alice Prior

Queen Elizabeth I, 110, 111

Queen Mary I, 3

Richard Mather, 107, 109, 110, 186

Richard Saltonstall, 5, 21

Richardson, Douglas. *See* Douglas Richardson

Robert Charles Anderson, 37

Robert Gorges, 19

Places

Amsterdam, Holland, 1
Bocking, 94, 95
Boston, 2, xii, xxiii, xxiv, xxv, xxvi, xxviii, xxix, 11, 19, 20, 23, 39, 46, 48, 49, 57, 99, 100, 117, 121, 123, 135, 136, 137, 144, 155, 158, 159, 161, 166, 167, 170, 175, 176, 199, 200, 203, 204, 205, 206, 207, 208, 209, 210, 212, 213, 214
Bristol, ix, 50, 208
Brookline, xii
Broxborune, 74
Bury St. Edmunds, 22
Cambridge, 3, 4, 7, 22, 42, 66, 112, 136, 137, 158, 175, 205, 206, 209, 211
Charles River, 136, 158
Charleston, 48, 51, 117, 121, 165
Cheshunt, 73, 75, 79, 82
Clipsham, 23
Commonwealth, 1
Concord, 48
Connecticut, xii, 137
Darenth, 49, 50, 51, 63, 208
Dedham, xii, 48, 117, 137, 143, 144, 145, 149, 158
Dorchester, xii, 9, 20, 44, 46, 48, 49, 57, 101, 107, 110, 117, 121, 130, 150, 153, 165, 178
England, 2, iii, iv, vii, viii, ix, xi, xii, xiv, xv, xvi, xvii, xviii, xix, xxiii, xxxi, xxxii, 1, 2, 3, 4, 6, 7, 8, 9, 10, 14, 15, 19, 20, 21, 22, 23, 24, 25, 26, 27, 28, 29, 31, 32, 33, 36, 37, 39, 41, 42, 47, 48, 49, 50, 51, 53, 54, 55, 56, 57, 58, 61, 62, 63, 64, 65, 66, 67, 99, 101, 102, 103, 104, 107, 110, 111, 112, 113, 117, 118, 119, 121, 122, 124, 129, 130, 133, 139, 153, 167, 170, 175, 179, 187, 189, 190, 193, 194, 195, 199, 200, 201, 203, 204, 205, 206, 207, 208, 209, 210, 211, 212, 213
Essex, vii, ix, 21, 26, 44, 47, 56, 57, 69, 70, 74, 75, 78, 79, 82, 85, 86, 88, 90, 92, 93, 94, 95, 97, 102, 103, 105, 115, 199, 203, 211, 212
Essex County, Massachusetts, vii, 199
First Burying Ground of Roxbury, xii, xxx
Great Amwell, 2, vii, xi, xviii, xix, 8, 9, 28, 39, 40, 42, 43, 44, 54, 55, 79, 81, 82, 91, 102, 103, 104, 112, 113, 209
Greater East Anglia, xi, xiii
Herne Hill, 50, 64, 65
Hertford, 47, 72, 73, 78, 80, 81, 82, 209
Hertford Hundred, 72
Hertfordshire, vii, viii, ix, xi, xiv, xv, xviii, xix, 42, 44, 47, 51, 53, 54, 55, 56, 62, 66, 67, 69, 70, 72, 73, 78, 79, 82, 91, 101, 102, 103, 104, 111, 133, 209, 211
Hoddesdon, 8, 77, 80
Jamestown, 20
Kent, 50, 51, 63, 64, 65, 68
Langton, 65
Lea Valley, 41
Lincolnshire, ix, xii, 22, 23, 62, 65, 68, 72, 210
London, ix, xi, 9, 20, 21, 22, 26, 28, 31, 40, 41, 42, 43, 50, 51, 55, 68, 70, 77, 79, 83, 84, 85, 86, 87, 88, 89, 92, 110, 113, 119, 120, 121, 122, 170, 172, 200, 203, 205, 206, 208, 211, 212, 213
Lynn, 7, 103, 105, 165, 211
Maine, xii
Massachusetts, 1, 2, vii, viii, ix, x, xi, xii, xxiv, xxvi, xxxi, xxxii, 1, 2, 3, 4, 6, 10, 12, 14, 15, 16, 19, 21, 22, 23, 25, 28, 29, 31, 32, 36, 37, 39, 42, 44,

41183862R00146

Made in the USA
Middletown, DE
05 March 2017